Not so Bad

by

Tudor Robins

Tudor Robins
www.tudorrobins.com

Publisher's Note: This is a work of fiction. Names, characters, places, and incidents are a product of the author's imagination. Locales and public names are sometimes used for atmospheric purposes. Any resemblance to actual people, living or dead, or to businesses, companies, events, institutions, or locales is completely coincidental.

Book Layout © 2017 BookDesignTemplates.com

Not so Bad / Tudor Robins -- 1st ed.
ISBN 978-1-990802-24-9 (ebook)
ISBN 978-1-990802-25-6 (paperback)
ISBN 978-1-990802-26-3 (hardcover)
ISBN 978-1-990802-27-0 (dust-jacketed hardcover)

Other Books by Tudor Robins:

Island Series:

Six-Month Horse (Prequel)
Wednesday Riders (Book Two)
Join Up (Book Three)
Faults (Book Four)
Reason Why (Book Five)

Stonegate Series:

Objects in Mirror (Book One)
After Lucas (Book Two)
Throw Your Heart Over (Book Three)

Perryside Series:

Moving North (Book One)

Mystery Stables:

Stolen Saddles (Book One)

Stand-Alones:

Meant to Be (Young Adult)
Before & After (Women's Fiction)
Not so Bad (Women's Fiction / Small-Town Romance)
In Search Of (Small-Town Romance)
Gift Horse (Holiday Novella)

One

I'VE BEEN THINKING about home all the time lately.

Is it even home when I haven't lived there for a decade? When it's 4,000 kilometres away? When two days after graduating from high school I crammed everything I owned into a ten-year-old Honda Civic and pulled onto the 401 without looking back?

It's the open-water swimming that fills me with nostalgia. I stand, goggled up and sucked into a compression bathing suit. Sun bathes the freckled skin of my shoulders. The wooden dock is warm underneath my bare feet. I'm about to jump out toward the blue of the sky, and land in the blue of the water.

Forget years, or distance, the sensations spin me straight back.

It's true the public swim raft is much bigger than any dock I grew up with — built to serve a beach that attracts thousands of people every day. And, yes, it floats, anchored in the bay instead of being attached to a cottage-country shoreline. Unlike the casual swim sessions of my childhood, a lifeguard with a city-issued vest scans the water. But the wood still thumps under my running feet as I launch myself off the end.

Hot skin hits cold water. The air whooshes out of my full lungs. I shoot to the surface, shake my head, and spit out a mouthful of water.

Salt water.

Wrong. This is all wrong. It's not home at all.

It happens every week — the building anticipation that comes of all my senses telling me this is just like home, it's exactly how I remember it — except, of course, for my sense of taste that tells me very clearly, no it's not.

I come back, though, because of those memory-laden before moments.

Also because participating in this weekly open-water swim gives me a legitimate reason for being late for the torture of Sunday brunch.

Treading (salt)water won't get me to the buoy moored 500 metres out, so I put my face back in the dreaded saltwater and swim.

I used to think the brunch was fun. Or, at least, I used to think it would start being fun.

Kind of like how when I got engaged to Tom, I thought I'd start falling in love with him.

I sigh, which messes up my breathing rhythm, which makes me choke on more of the offensive saltwater.

Ugh. It's going to be another wasted Sunday.

***

Maybe I was too pessimistic. The sun's out, after all, without a hint of fog – always a bonus on the West Coast.

I think my hair might be drying with beach waves. It's a look I'll never be able to replicate, but I might as well enjoy it for now.

It's past mid-morning and I still don't have any urgent texts or emails from my boss, meaning none of our reputationally challenged clients did anything really dumb last night — or at least, if they did, they haven't remembered it yet — so I don't have to clean up after other people's late-night binges, be they substance, sex, or social media in nature.

"Hey, Happy!"

And JJ's on his corner.

He's safe, he looks clean, he's smiling. "Are you hungry?" I ask.

"I wouldn't say no," he says.

"I'm already late for brunch, but if you come to Timmie's with me, you can pick what you want."

"I don't want to make you later than you already are," he says.

He isn't suggesting I don't treat him to food. He's suggesting I give him the money instead. One day in a moment of weakness, or strength — I'm not sure which — he told me, "I'd rather have the cash so I can go to the liquor store, which is exactly why you shouldn't give it to me."

I look him right in the eye. "I offered. Are you coming?" JJ's smart; he knows what I'm saying.

He hooks his arm through mine. "Nothing I'd rather do."

I wish everyone was as easy to talk to as JJ. I know some people — OK, most people — think I'm curt. Sometimes rude. But if they picked up on things, I wouldn't have to be. Most people know the score early in a conversation, but they'll push and push until I'm forced to tell them what I really think.

Which is sometimes ... *blunt.*

JJ's also the only person who calls me "Happy."

And, for a brief interlude after loading him up with a hot coffee, a farmer's wrap, and a Boston cream donut, I'm happy to the core. I'm a person who makes other people happy. I embody happiness.

I'm hit by another rush of nostalgia when I see a big, dirt-splashed pickup parked along the curb. It's a rare sight here in my very trendy neighbourhood, but it whirls me right back to the rural community where I grew up. Where we had to transport hay and tow livestock trailers, and an electric two-seater Fiat just wouldn't cut it.

Even though it gives me a pang, it's not a bad memory. I had my first kiss — in fact, I had almost all my high school kisses — in trucks not unlike this one, so my happiness stays intact.

Until I near the restaurant and spot my fiancé's Range Rover parked on the road with its unmistakable **WNR WNR** personalized license plate. Cringe.

There are five of them sitting in the prime spot on the patio. Tom, his best-man-to-be, Brady who plays in the NHL, and his future groomsman Hunter, host of the city's most-listened to radio morning show, occupy one corner of the table, with a seat left empty for me beside Brady's fiancée Chantal, and Yasmin, who got married to Hunter in Lake Como earlier this year.

At any patio table there's always one seat in the glaring sun – the one left for me is it.

I reach over to manoeuvre the patio umbrella into a tilt, which blocks most of the sun from my intended seat.

Yasmin protests. "Hey! Now the sun's on me."

"On your *shoulder*," I say. "So now you have five percent of the sun instead of me having one hundred percent of it."

She snaps back. "You were one hundred percent late."

"You all knew I was swimming. I asked if you wanted to shift brunch and you said no. Suck it up."

Chantal sighs. "You don't have to always remind us of your great prowess as an open-water swimmer, Hazel. Your hair tells the story."

I lift my hand to those beach waves I was so proud of. The texture is more than a little crunchy. My pinky sticks as I pull my fingers through my hair. There's a strand of dried seaweed stuck to my thumb.

"Well, at least the state of *my* hair's temporary."

Chantal gasps — with good reason. It's a low blow. The lowest, really.

Several weeks ago, Chantal called me in tears. She'd been to her stylist in preparation for a charity gala she was going to with Brady and insisted that her hair needed to be platinum.

It had gone very wrong. Chunks of her hair were falling out. The gala was in four hours.

Doing reputation-rescue for celebrities gives me a crazy network of contacts. Including a wig designer. I had Chantal gala-ready with time to spare.

Then I sent her an invoice for my time.

That's what gives me the pang about alluding to the wig which — unless her hair has had a miraculous recovery — she's wearing today. Chantal and I might not be true friends, but I secured Chantal that wig as a client, and I owe my clients the utmost in discretion.

Yasmin's looking confused, as well she should. The wig is gorgeous. You can't tell it's not real hair because it *is* real hair. At the first group brunch post-gala, Chantal made a point of declaring that her stylist had used a special serum on her hair before Yasmin could ask about the newfound thick, bouncy, shininess of Chantal's locks.

At every get-together since, I've been entertained by Yasmin trying to weasel the details out of Chantal, while Chantal comes up with new and more outrageous excuses for not sharing the name of the serum. "My stylist compounds it herself," "It costs more per ounce than platinum," and, finally, when those didn't work, "It's made with a type of fungus that only grows in the Camargue, in France, for three weeks in the spring and my stylist can't get any more until next year."

Yasmin might not understand why my comment has caused Chantal's face to blanch, accompanied by rapid blinking, which has Brady turning to her asking, "What? What is it?" but Tom's onto me.

He's by my side in a few quick seconds, and takes advantage of the fact that I still haven't sat down to cup my elbow — forcefully — in his hand and guide me — firmly — to the railing at the edge of the patio. "What did you do?"

A quick glance tells me Chantal is full-on crying now — anything for attention — so there's no point saying,

"Nothing." Instead, I give him a hard stare. "Why do you care?"

"Because, as you well know, if she's not happy, he's not allowed to be happy, and if you're the cause of her not being happy, that puts a lot of things in jeopardy for me."

It's true there are many perks to being the best friend of an NHL player — especially one that lucked onto a Grey-Cup winning team as a late-season trade. Between Brady and Hunter, Tom never has to pay for a round of golf or concert tickets, and always has somebody's expensive summer home to escape to on weekends when the city is at its stifling worst.

You could say I enjoy the same perks, except I'm not sure I've ever *enjoyed* time spent with know-it-all Yasmin, or narcissistic Chantal, or self-important Hunter. Brady's the best of the bunch — he'd be a pretty normal guy if his whole life didn't revolve around chasing a small projectile made of rubber around a sheet of ice, but he's so quiet his presence never changes the dynamic much.

And Tom — do I enjoy time spent with my fiancé?

Before I can think too hard about it, a voice distracts me. "Hey, Happy!"

Shit. I hate that my first reaction to seeing JJ is negative, but having JJ and Tom in the same place is a collision of two worlds that can't go well.

"Who is that?" Although he's looking at me, Tom is clearly not at all interested in my answer since he immediately turns to JJ. "Who are you? Why are you talking to my fiancé? What's your problem?"

JJ lifts his hands, lurches slightly, and winks at me. "Who's the one with the problem? I don't think it's me."

"Oh, buddy ..." Tom steps away from me and right up to the fence. "Keep on like that, and you are *so* going to have a problem. Even bigger than the substance abuse problem you obviously already have."

"Tom!"

"Sorry, Hazel, but aren't you the one who tells the hard truths even when people don't want to hear them? Isn't 'honesty the best policy?'" He hooks quotes into the air as he says this. He's never let it go since that one time I told him he had halitosis. "Your friend here is drunk. As a skunk. Loaded. Swimming in booze."

More likely high, I'm guessing, since JJ seemed sober when I left him at Timmies — it would have been hard for him to drink enough to be swaying the way he is in that short time span. But it's not an argument I'm going to get into with Tom.

"Stop it, Tom."

"Yeah," JJ slurs. "Tom, stop it."

It all happens so fast. Tom lurches for the fence. JJ leaps back. The fence gives way, Tom sprawls, staff members rush, patrons stare, Yasmin yells, "I'm calling the police!" and Chantal sobs through it all.

I look down at my feet. I look up at the sky. I look out at JJ's rapidly retreating back. Then I leave.

* * *

The sidewalk is busy and I merge into the flow of people. Everybody dresses pretty much the same on these warm days in the summer. From the back I'm sure I don't stand out. Cropped jeans, a black halter top, those beach waves ... or tangled nest, dependent on your outlook, I guess. Even my wet swimming gear doesn't give me away since it's stowed in a sealed dry bag inside a big, leather tote.

I don't hurry away from the restaurant. Don't rush. Just let my feet go and my mind wander as I listen to the conversations around me:

"... he was bored in math class so he climbed out of the window. I mean, what do you do with a kid like that?"

"... wondering what he's going to think when he realizes I didn't invite his sister ..."

I wonder what Tom will think when he notices I'm not at the restaurant.

"... sometimes I wonder when she's going to grow up."

I wonder *when* Tom will notice I'm not there.

The two people in front of me are laughing so hard one loses her balance and falls against her friend.

I try to remember the last time I laughed with a friend like that. I try not to admit the answer is probably never.

My phone buzzes. OK, I wouldn't have put money on Tom noticing this quickly.

The text isn't from Tom, though. It's from his neighbour — recently divorced and unwilling to get an actual job in case it affects her alimony payments, but always looking for cash jobs to do. Tom pays her to let the dog out when he's away all day, or works late. So, pretty much every day. **I texted Tom but he's not answering** the neighbour writes. **That little shit bit me again. I'm done. I'm not even trying to get that devil creature back in her crate. She's loose in the house. Don't say I didn't tell you.**

Great.

Truth — I'm not a big fan of the dog. She wasn't my idea. In fact, I tried to talk Tom out of taking her. Many times. But his boss asked him to look after her, "just for a while." Right before leaving to live with a mountain guide, his wife had bought something called a "doxiepoo" – the unique-looking offspring of a poodle and a dachshund – from a mall pet store as a consolation gift for their daughter.

The dog bit the daughter.

The daughter didn't want the dog, but didn't want anything to happen to the dog. "You'll take her, right?" the boss asked Tom.

"You work more hours than him." I'd pointed out. "You have no clue about dogs. She bites."

"It's temporary, and it will get me brownie points."

It had been temporary four months ago and, since then, the boss had moved to a Denver law firm. Spending ten hours a day in a crate, only let out by Tom's neighbour, hadn't helped the dog's biting problem. Obviously.

It's not her fault, though. I know that.

I also know, loose in the house, she'll find Tom's Salvatore Ferragamo loafers and eat them.

I sigh. Then I turn right instead of left at the next block — heading for Tom's place instead of mine.

***

The dog is, indeed, loose.

She's also delighted to see me to the extent that she loses all bladder control. I'm aware Tom thinks less of her for peeing every time she sees me, and — for some reason — less of me for prompting that reaction in her.

I don't know why, of all people in the world, she likes me, but there it is. It makes me feel sad for a second — what will she do once I'm gone?

Then I catch myself — once I'm gone? *Where? When? What do I mean?*

I shake the question off, and scoop the dog off the floor so I can carry her across the room and to the sliding doors that open onto Tom's tiny backyard.

With her outside, nose pressed against the glass, I shoo her off — "Go pee!" — then set about cleaning up the pee she already did inside, checking her food and water, and while I'm filling up her water bowl, a funny thing happens.

My eye falls on a shallow bowl I placed on the windowsill above Tom's sink so I'd always have a safe place to slip off any jewelry I was wearing while I did the dishes.

I love that little bowl. It's the twin of one I have on my own windowsill. They were keepsakes I got when my favourite great-aunt died.

I pick up the bowl and drop it into my bag.

Then I start a slow walk through the townhouse.

The dog hurls herself at the patio doors as I walk by.

There isn't much, but what there is, I'd be sad to lose.

I leave the toothbrush in the bathroom — it's time for a new one, anyway — but I take the small bottle of overpriced lubricating eye drops my optometrist has me hooked on. I snag the light bathrobe hanging on the back of Tom's bedroom door; I've always liked it better than the one I have at home.

The hardest decision is about the little painting in the front hall. We bought it together on a trip to the Okanagan, but it's always hung here.

I reach out, touch the frame, begin to lift it off the hook, then shake my head. It looks right here, in BC, but I'm going to Ontario.

Again, I wonder where the thought came from.

Except it feels right. I'm going to Ontario. I suddenly know it.

With my bag overstuffed I let the dog back in. When I show her the crate, her tail drops between her legs, but she goes, then immediately turns around and stares at me as though she knows. "Take me, too," she might as well be saying.

I think of all the shoes she's eaten, and her yippy little bark, and I shake my head. "You wouldn't survive half a day on the farm."

So, that's it — apparently I'm not just going to Ontario, I'm going to the farm.

I'm quite sure it's my heart that's made this decision, not my head. Let's face it — my heart's been running the show all day. My little bursts of nostalgia haven't come from my usually logical, cool, rational brain.

I don't know where they're from, and I'm not quite comfortable with them, but they're in me right now and they're filling me with a reckless excitement at the thought of getting out of here, and packing up my car and retracing that long drive across Canada.

And leaving my key to Tom's house here.

My hand's already working at the key ring, even as my head's asking, *Is this a good idea?*

"Ow!" The key ring pinches my finger, but if anything it strengthens my resolve. My heart is determined this stupid key ring isn't going to stop me.

Head: What if I change my mind?

Heart: I'll just say I left it here by mistake.

Head: That it — what? — fell off the key chain?

Heart: Obviously not, since the damn thing's so stubborn it's now broken my nail ... but, yeah, Tom doesn't need to know that. I can say it fell off.

Head: Do you think he's stupid?

Heart: No. Not stupid. But also not very nice.

Head: Which was never a problem before.

Heart: Well, what can I say? I've been falling down on the job. I should have spoken up sooner.

Head: I wish you'd just stay quiet now.

The key's off and in my hand. I feel a little thrill of triumph, followed by a frisson of fear. But it's excitement-tinged fear.

It's the feeling of being alive, my heart says.

Oh, shut up, my head counters.

While they argue, I place the key on Tom's hall table, sling my bag over my shoulder, and open his front door, making sure the knob lock is set.

I take a deep breath before I pull it closed behind me. Once I'm out, I won't be able to get back in.

My eyes fall to the ring on my hand holding the door.

While I'm leaving things behind, maybe I should leave that too.

Before my head and heart can get into a fresh argument about that one, I yank the door shut.

I'm not feeling that emotional. The ring was expensive. The ring is quite beautiful. The ring was custom-made. For me. The ring is *mine.*

As I walk away, I twirl the ring on my finger and feel somewhat reassured that despite all the crazy things I've done today, I've held onto at least a small part of my practicality.

***

Before I leave, I try to find JJ.

I walk the streets swinging a 40-pack of Timbits as though it's a lunch box.

He's nowhere to be found.

Normally I wouldn't worry. Until now, JJ has been a presence I see sometimes on my way to work. I don't keep track of him. I'm sure he doesn't keep track of me.

But since my fiancé — ex-fiancé — lunged at him across a patio fence, I feel some obligation to find him.

I'm realizing I don't know much about the only person in the world who thinks I'm "happy."

The only places I know to look for him are along my walking route to work, and by the restaurant.

I go. I walk. There are crowds. There are cars, and buses. There are bicycles on the sidewalk that should be on the road. There's a kid weaving through pedestrians on a longboard. But I don't see an always-grinning, just-a-bit-taller-than-me guy with thick dark hair that gleams in the sunlight whenever the Vancouver clouds part enough to let it shine through.

I'm nearly back at my condo which I used to like fine, but now, juxtaposed against my nostalgic memories of the character farmhouse and lush countryside of my childhood seems soulless, boring, and far-too-expensive for a tiny space with a mediocre view.

The fruitless search for JJ, and the deeper questions of what I've been doing with my life — why I was engaged to a mean guy, with friends I don't even like, while living somewhere that's more hotel than home — has me dragging my heels, when I spot Belinda.

JJ introduced me to her once. To be honest, I was busy — running late for a meeting to figure out how to back a provincial politician out of some racist comments he'd made — so I didn't pay attention at the time, but seeing her now makes me exhale with relief.

"Belinda! It's me, Hazel, JJ's friend. Do you know where he is?"

She shakes her head. "Sorry. Haven't seen him today. Are those for him?"

I glance down at the box in my hand. "Um, yes …"

She holds her hand out. "I'll give them to him when I see him."

"I …" I hesitate. Can I trust her? Will she pass them on? It's not that I'm worried about the $7.99 box of treats, it's that I've also tucked a grocery store gift card inside, with a note:

JJ, I'm sorry about what happened. It was my fault. I need to pick my friends more carefully.

I'm leaving town for a while. I hope this might help you out. Here's my email if you ever need anything.

The fingers on the woman's outstretched hand are adorned with beautiful hand-poked tattoos. She has a kind smile.

"Thank you," I say, and hand the box over. After all, there's a very good chance JJ's friends are much better than my own.

Two

I'M SITTING in a harvest gold plastic chair outside unit 7B of the Nearly There Motel. The chair isn't old enough to be vintage, or new enough to be retro — it's just ugly. Yet, like the boxy television in the room, it's chained to the wall.

A paint-peeling sign declaring **MOTEL** and promising TV, Air, Heat, and Vacancy stands against a background of sharp Rocky Mountain peaks rising as far as the eye can see.

It's very Canadian to have such an abundance of beauty that we don't have to be precious about it.

It's Sunday night and I'm so close to the Alberta border I could get there on foot, meaning even if I started driving back now, I'd have trouble getting to work by 9:00 tomorrow morning.

And I have no desire to head back.

I should email work. I should call Tom. I should send a message to my brother.

I don't do any of those things. I also don't open a book, or go inside to turn on the ancient television.

I just sit, and let the light go grainy and turn to night. Dark things swoop through the air. Finally I have to slap at the first mosquito — another very Canadian experience — then I return to my room and fall asleep.

**

During my eight-plus hours of driving between the Nearly There Motel and the Halfway Inn (located in Saskatchewan, halfway between Swift Current and Moose Jaw according to the woman who checks me in), I accumulate five missed calls from my boss, Devon.

Settled into a chair almost identical to yesterday's — except this one is orange-brown — I discover Devon has also sent a few emails. On the grounds that it's the most relevant, I read the latest one.

Where the eff are you? It's not that Devon's too polite to use the real word, it's that he doesn't want his messages to end up in the spam folder. **I've had that piece of work, Belinda Rothman, calling me all day. Lily's decided to apply to med school. We need to fast forward the reputation reconstruct.**

If Lily Rothman wants to be a doctor, she should know what parts of her anatomy show when she dances on a speaker in Ibiza with no underwear on. No flashing of the Rothman undercarriage = no need for a reputation reconstruct.

When I have to identify my industry on any kind of application, I select "marketing" but Devon's firm doesn't market products or services — we market people. When he's not worried about spam filters, Devon says, "You fuck up, we fix it."

Which, essentially, means most of my clients are terrible people. Devon's not particularly pleasant, either. I fit right in, and the pay is good, which means I should want to keep the job, Still, I can't make myself care enough to send a useful answer about Belinda Rothman and her entitled daughter.

Instead I lie. **Devon,** I type. **I have appendicitis. I'm scheduled for an emergency appendectomy tomorrow. They told me to take two weeks off work. I'll update you when I know more.**

Which leaves me just enough energy to text my brother: **Brody, I'm coming to Ontario. I'll be there Wednesday, late. See you Thursday morning.**

Then I spend a long time staring at the kind of immense blue sky you just don't see in BC. With no mountains to interrupt it, it goes on, and on, and on.

It's beautiful, just like BC's mountains are beautiful, but neither of them is home, so I'm going to need to keep driving.

The couple staying in the next room come out to sit in their plastic chairs. They have a bottle of wine and the plastic-wrapped cups from the bathroom. They smile at me.

I'm seized by a sudden fear that they're going to invite me to join them, so I make an exaggerated slap at a lazy mosquito and go inside, where I'm asleep before the sun's fully down.

***

The next night's motel is within spitting distance of the Ontario border. This one's tucked into the edge of the boreal forest and faces a hulking rock cut displaying an enormous chunk of Canadian Shield.

I would sit and admire it, but there's no chair in front of my unit — I suspect the people two doors down of stealing it — how else would they get three avocado green chairs in front of their room? I perch on the step with the door pressing against my back while I connect to the guest WiFi.

Devon's sent a message. **I suppose you can't help the appendix thing, but now the Rothmans also want us to write Lily's med school application essay. They asked for you specifically.**

I think of telling him to do it himself. I think of referring him to the legal duty to accommodate employees suffering illness under the BC labour code. I think of telling him to eff off.

Ultimately, though, given that this would be the day of my fictitious surgery, I simply don't answer.

There's no reply from my brother, which doesn't surprise me. The only technology he likes is the computer in his smart tractor.

There is a message from Tom. There have been lots of text messages and voicemails from him — none of which I've read or listened to. He's obviously decided to try email as a last resort. His name is bold and so is the subject line, **What the actual fuck?** That's pretty much in line with the text messages I've ignored so far.

Considering I left Vancouver because of the lightbulb realization that my fiancé was not a very nice person, these messages aren't doing much to change my mind.

I turn off my devices, pull the blackout curtains tight against the still-light summer evening, and crawl into bed.

Drive and sleep. Drive and sleep. It's what I've decided to do. It's all I can focus on. If I linger anywhere, if I slow down, if I don't download enough podcasts to fill my driving hours, I'm afraid I'll think.

I'm not quite halfway there, and if I think too hard I might turn around and go back.

And even though I'm not sure what I want to do, I'm pretty sure going back isn't it.

* * *

I thought everything would be the same.

I expected it to mirror the pictures that have been flashing through my head since that weird day back in Vancouver — the ones that drew me back here.

The 401 is the same of course — a divided highway with most of the interest safetied out of it so the final two hours of highway driving feels longer than many of the drawn-out days of driving I've already put in.

I force myself to stay awake and alert, though. Even as the sun slants low into my eyes. Even as I get boxed in by towering transport trucks.

Because I'm almost there and it's been an effort, and a journey, and a commitment, and a trek. I've crossed more than half the country — this huge country. I don't want to mark it with an encounter with the rumble strip, a tree, or a transport truck.

Stay awake.

The exit sign is different.

It's reflective — popping out in the beams of passing headlights despite the gathering gloom. It says **Visit the County — next three exits** and it boasts a unique and catchy logo that looks like it was created by an actual design firm.

What's going on?

When I take the exit, there are more differences. Many trees are noticeably taller. One towering oak is gone. The road is wider and the pavement smoother. There are new houses with three-car garages. There are more new signs touting local attractions — mostly wineries and art galleries; at least that hasn't changed.

It's disconcerting, though, to have fled my old life drawn by a powerful tug of nostalgia only to find the place I was pulled to has gone ahead and changed without me.

Fortunately the school bus shelter from my school days is still in its spot at the end of the driveway, to confirm that even if the neighbour's fence appears to have collapsed under its own weight, and the mailbox is on the other side of the road, this is the farm.

Although ... I frown as my headlights sweep over the wooden structure ... there's something different.

The yawn that seizes me is so violent I can't see ahead for several seconds. I stop thinking about bus shelters, and squint through the last grainy bit of post-sunset light for the trailer that's spent as long as I can remember sagging and rusting on the same spot.

My appearance-obsessed mother allowed it to stay there as a deterrent against too-long visits from family members on my dad's side – even if my bachelor uncle felt right at home surrounded by orange-and-brown (and very dusty) polyester curtains, and indoor-outdoor turf carpeting, there were only so many days his back could take the springs poking through the ancient mattress.

When I get inside, I'm both surprised and relieved to find the trailer transformed to a neat, tidy, even stylish space. I have no nostalgia for the stale smell it always held, or the flypaper twists hanging from the ceiling.

I'm almost too tired to go back out to the car for my bag. I stare at myself in the tiny bathroom mirror and wonder would it be worse to navigate the few steps back and forth to the car right now, or to wake up with furry teeth.

I notice there's a new toothbrush on the edge of the sink, with a travel-sized tube of toothpaste.

Decision made.

I lie down on a firm mattress made up with crisp sheets and run my tongue around my minty mouth. The last thing I think is that I've never known another smell I like as much as the aroma of fresh-cut hay drifting through the window screen of the trailer.

Then I'm gone.

Three

I OPEN ONE EYE. The one the sun's not slanting across. Outside the trailer window — which let in those fresh-cut hay smells all night — there's a shifting kaleidoscope of hazy green. Leaves fluttering in the breeze. There's chirping and singing outside — birds, insects, frogs — I can't distinguish, but it's pretty. Half my body's in sunlight warm enough to make me very lazy; not hot enough for discomfort. The firm mattress feels just as good as when I first lay down on it.

I close the eye again. I'm not ready to be awake. I'm not even sure if I have a job anymore — less sure if I care. As far as my fiancé — *former* fiancé — is concerned I'm ... well, the last subject line I saw from him said something about **completely crazy**. I'm pretty sure my brother and sister-in-law would be happy not to see me until noon. Or, not to see me at all. In other words, there's no reason why I have to be awake.

Which is great. It means I can drift.

Except for my goddamn bladder.

Really? Seriously? I was borderline dehydrated when I went to bed last night. My water bottle was empty, and I had no idea whether the water in the trailer was potable. It wasn't back in the days when the mattress was an instrument of torture and the place smelled like ass.

So what, exactly, does my body need to pee out now?

I shift and there's no denying it — I need to go.

Also, with that discomfort raising its demanding hand, my stomach starts growling. No water last night, and no food either, and my body's complaining about it.

This time I open both eyes and notice a note propped on the tiny counter by the miniscule sink. *Hazel.*

Between my screaming bladder, my grumbling stomach, and the note promising *Coffee and breakfast in the farmhouse,* I guess I'm getting up.

I push myself to a sitting position and think it's unfair for somebody who just had an appendectomy — even if it was imaginary — to be getting up this early.

***

The screen door. That's the sure sign I'm back in rural Ontario. Screen doors signify trust that nobody's going to break into your house, and country breezes blowing through the house.

These are not things I'm used to in the city.

Then again, they also signify bugs to be kept outside and no air conditioning.

The other thing screen doors are good for is standing outside them and listening to what's going on inside the house.

Which, right now, in my childhood home, is water running, dishes clattering, and my sister-in-law's frazzled voice. "Patrick, why are you still eating? What's taking you so long?"

"He's sorting his marshmallows." I'm pretty sure that's my oldest niece, Violet.

"He's what?"

"He'll only eat his marshmallows in order. You know: pink hearts, yellow moons ..."

"Are you kidding me? Patrick, what are you going to do when you have to catch the bus again?"

"But I don't have to catch the bus today, Mom."

"You still can't spend the entire morning fishing a yellow moon out of your cereal bowl — if you're not done in four minutes, you'll be having plain oatmeal for the rest of your life. Where's Ali?"

"Changing." Violet's voice again.

"Of course." There's something new in Aggie's voice I can't nail down. Almost a sadness. "What about you, Violet?"

"I'm done, Mom. My bowl's in the dishwasher and I can get a start on the chicken coop. I'll go get ..." She comes into the hallway. She's so much taller than I expected. I give a tiny gasp and she turns to the door and squeals, "It's Auntie Hazel!" She yanks the door open and with the haze of the screen gone I'm faced with bright eyes, high cheekbones with freckles across them, a smile higher on one side than the other, and ears that stick out just enough so they show through her hair.

Myself, when I was younger. It's a shock how much she looks like me.

I hope she's nicer.

She steps out and wraps her arms around me. Presses her head sideways against me and mumbles, "We're so glad you're here."

Definitely nicer than me.

There's a cowlick at the crown of her head and that, along with the boniness of her chin resting on my arm, flares the nostalgia feeling again. Even though I've never seen this child at this stage in her development before. Still, there it is.

I pull my eyes away from the swirl of my niece's hair to lock eyes with my sister-in-law who's stepped into the kitchen doorway. The tea towel she's holding is a reminder I've interrupted her. "Hi Hazel," she says.

"Hi Aggie."

She turns sideways. "Come on in. You must be hungry."

Hunger. In the morning. It's a very unfashionable thing to admit to in my office. You're supposed to say, "All I need is a litre of coffee," and you're supposed to brew it strong and drink it black. It's just the first in a long list of rules to observe every day so it will be clear you're tough, and with-it, and worthy of working in an open-plan loft where everyone sits on either a yoga ball or a bean bag chair.

When I step inside, the same round table we used to sit at during my childhood comes into view and in the middle of it are a box of Weetabix, a box of Corn Flakes, and a box of Lucky Charms.

Oh, fuck the black coffee. "I'll have some Lucky Charms." I reach for the box, only to encounter resistance. Patrick. My nephew. Both hands on the Lucky Charms box safeguarding his orange stars.

I lift one eyebrow. He does it, too.

I don't spend a lot of time with kids, but I'm pretty sure the gracious — the adult — thing to do when a nine-year-old doesn't want you to eat their special treat cereal, is not to do it.

I want the cereal even more now than I did before he started tug-of-warring me for it.

I relax my grip and his eyebrow lowers, which is when I give a sudden yank. "Ah-ha!"

He wrinkles his nose and narrows his eyes. "Mom was right about you."

What the hell? I shoot a glance at my sister-in-law, elbow-deep in dishwater — I'm almost positive another adult thing to do is not to bad-mouth relatives in front of your nine-year-old.

Before I can get into it with her, the screen door bangs, followed by the clump-clump of heavy boots stomping inside, then two muffled bangs as they get kicked off onto the mat.

Sounds, smells, images, memories — why are they suddenly so vivid? Why won't they leave me alone?

I swallow hard. *It's not my dad.*

Even though when I was a nine-year-old sitting at this table, that's just how it sounded when he came in.

This isn't then. We didn't have Lucky Charms then, for one thing. I give my head a half-shake and — cereal box clutched against my chest — lock eyes with the person who just came in. "Hey Brodes."

His smile is broad and genuine. For a second it looks like he's going to hug me, then he looks at the Lucky Charms box and ruffles his son's head instead. "Isn't it nice to have Auntie Hazel here, bud?"

My nephew makes a growling noise which is cut off by my sister-in-law's voice slicing across it, "Patrick!"

The warning's unmistakable, as is the strength of her order which she issues without turning away from her sink full of dishes, "Go help your sister clean the chicken coop."

There's a stray marshmallow on the table which my nephew picks up, and eyes fixed on me, pops it into his mouth to crunch between his teeth before scuttling out of the room.

Oh, the crunchy deliciousness of Lucky Charms marshmallows. Now I need to find a bowl ...

Brody wanders over to his wife and bumps his hip against hers. She turns her head and shoots him a smile so brief I could have imagined it, except it's also so affectionate that it shoots a spear of jealousy through me. No nostalgia trigger here. Tom's never smiled at me that way — nobody's ever smiled at me that way — although, to be fair I've never given anyone a smile like that, either.

"It's great you're here, Haze," my brother says. "We didn't think we'd see you until the wedding."

I'm pouring cereal when he says it, and my hand jerks and sends a precious green clover skittering toward the edge of the table. *The wedding.*

"Shit!"

"*Language,*" Aggie snaps. "There are kids in the house."

TUDOR ROBINS

Two things. The stomping and banging from upstairs tell me no kids are in earshot, and if she thinks her kids haven't heard that word before … I open my mouth to make both points and Brody slides between us — both physically and conversationally. "'Shit,' what, Haze?"

Aggie shoots him a look.

"OK, 'sugar' what, Hazel?"

"Um, about the wedding — have you booked your flights yet?"

Aggie's back stiffens, shoulders hike. She flashes another scowl at Brody. He speaks, "We will. We're just waiting for a seat sale."

"Phew! That's a relief." I pop the marshmallow in my mouth. "Don't bother. We're not getting married."

Aggie whirls around, hands still dripping. "Since when?"

I shrug. "I was pretty darn sure when I drove out of Vancouver. By the time I got to the Ontario-Manitoba border I was completely convinced."

"For god's sake, Hazel, how can you be so flip? People are just expendable to you. Nobody matters."

I remember this room, this house, this farm, when my dad was still alive. When everything mattered.

Then I remember the time after … and since. When the only way to get through — for me, anyway — was to make sure nothing did.

• 40 •

And now? The twinges that brought me back here? What are they?

They're scary — that's what.

I can enjoy a quick visit. I can take a break, catch my breath, get this sentimentality out of my system.

I just can't let my guard down.

I meet my disapproving sister-in-law's eyes and give a deliberate shrug. "Whatever you say."

After all, she's the one who said I was flip.

***

It's not like Aggie ever liked me, so why should that change now? And why should it bother me? The answer is, it doesn't. Of course it doesn't.

It's fine. She can do her and I'll do me.

Having said that, I also don't feel like running into her again today.

Going into the village would be one obvious way to avoid her, but that idea comes with its own pitfalls.

First, it would involve me getting back in the car, and driving. Cradling the cup of brewed coffee I brought back from the farmhouse kitchen, I peer through the window of the trailer out at my dusty little hatchback. Back in Vancouver it was a city dweller's toy. Small enough to park in the tightest urban spots, its rounded outline and lime green paint job made it look like a candy — bright, peppy, and appealing.

Here it looks dirty, flimsy, and out-of-place.

I flex my right hand and a twinge runs up my arm to my elbow. And, yes, 4,500 kilometres of gripping the steering wheel and shifting gears has given me tendinitis.

So, I'm not driving today.

Also, considering last I checked the village's population was 171, there's a very good chance I'd run into my mother while trying to avoid Aggie.

Which would very much be a case of out of the frying pan, into the fire.

I'm contemplating my options which seem to be go for a run, or a walk, or a hike — something on foot, anyway — or stay in the trailer and continue to drink coffee. Except I'd have to switch to instant, because a quick glance in the cupboard tells me that's all there is in the kitchenette.

Another cupboard reveals non-dairy creamer.

I could get fired from my job for drinking instant coffee with non-dairy creamer in it. If I still have a job when I recover from my not-appendectomy, that is.

Don't think about that now ...

All to say, fake-coffee-in-the-trailer isn't going to happen.

Something outdoors, then.

I'm bent over, reaching for my shoes, when there's a tap on the thin aluminum of the door, right at the height of my head.

When I open the door, there's a girl dressed in a swirl of bright fabric standing on the bottom step of the trailer. The morning breeze furls her turquoise skirt around her ankles. Her cropped baby pink top reveals a band of baby pink skin, and hair the same shade as Violet's tumbles around her face in soft, shiny curls.

I notice the tips of the ears peeking through the pretty hair. The freckles across the nose.

I put two and two together and hope I've got it right. "I saw your brother and sister, and I was wondering when I was going to see you."

The girl smiles. "Auntie Hazel?"

I nod.

"I'm Ali."

"I knew that's who you were."

"But you probably didn't know my name's Ali now."

"You're right. I didn't." Her name used to be Alex. She was Patrick's twin brother. Now I guess she's just Patrick's twin. "I think that name suits you."

"Thanks." She tilts her head to the side and, in stark contrast to her scowly brother, is all kinds of precious and adorable. It's faces like hers that make women my age get married and take long maternity leaves. "I thought of having an entirely new name but ..." She shrugs and manages to exude more charm, "... there are way too many names to choose from."

I nod. "I hear you." In fact, she's landed on the exact reason Tom's dog is still called, "The dog." Her name, in her previous life, was Muffkins.

By the end, Tom and I didn't agree on much, but we were in harmony with our flat-out refusal to call the dog "Muffkins." Unfortunately, neither of us could come up with a name that worked for her. So, "the dog" she is.

Or *was*. Is that right? She's not dead, but she's nothing to do with me anymore ...

"Aunt Hazel?"

"Yes, honey?"

"Were you thinking of something else?"

"Um, yes. I was. Sorry."

"That's OK. Mom says you're single-minded, but I don't see how anyone can be single-minded, really. There are so many things to think about."

What on earth has my sister-in-law been telling these kids about me?

Before I can do a deep dive into that question, I hear "Ali! Ali, where are you? You didn't help with the chicken coop and now ... Oh! Ali, you shouldn't be bugging Auntie Hazel. Mom says she's not so good with family relations."

OK, that's it. I may be many things, but I'm not passive aggressive. And it's precisely because I'm not, that I'm going to have a direct conversation with Aggie about these little gems my nieces and nephew keep dropping.

"Marta's here," Violet says.

Ali shrugs. "I'm not riding."

"Well, you still have to come to the barn. Mom's going grocery shopping and she says you need to be where we can see you while she's gone."

Violet turns to me. "She asked if you want to go with her. In case there's anything you want in the village."

I think of the ten-minute drive sitting next to my sister-in-law. I think of the possibility of running into my mother — not that she shops in the village grocery store; she has a long-running feud with the family that owns it — but 171 people. It could happen.

"Um. It's nice of her to ask, but ..."

"No!" Violet's voice is triumphant. "I knew you'd rather ride with us. I knew you wouldn't be able to wait any longer to see Quinte ... despite what Mom said."

Another Aggie diss. This time, it's hard to feel angry, though. This time what I feel is guilt — driven by the knowledge that, whatever, my sister-in-law said about me, when it comes to the way I treated Quin, she's probably right.

***

The kids want to show me their ponies. Well, OK, Violet wants to show me all their ponies. She leads me through the barn, stopping first at a cross-tied chestnut whose kind eyes and neat ears mark it as a Welsh pony, around 12.2.

"This is Milford. He was my pony, but he's Patrick's now." Her hand lingers on the lovely arched neck. Patrick allows that, but when I place my hand next to hers, he pulls the pony away and leads him into a small box stall. "I'm going to tack him up in here."

We move to the next stall. "This is Ali's pony, Cressy." I've never seen a more adorable pony than this one with her bright, long-lashed eyes and just the right balance of black points to lend emphasis to her beautiful dappled grey coat. "She's beautiful," I say.

"She's *fat*." Violet gives Ali a pointed stare. "Ali hasn't been on her yet this season. It's not good for her."

Ali blinks, then leans in and kisses the pony's neck. "I love her."

"Then ride her!" There's an exasperation in Violet's voice that makes her sound more like she's thirty-two than twelve. I wonder if this is something else she's overheard from her mother.

"Show her Banks," Ali says with something in her tone that tells me it's a way of getting back at her sister.

I follow Ali across the aisle, with Violet trailing, to the door of a stall that at first appears to be empty.

When we arrive, though, there's a rustle of bedding, then a flash as the light catches the eye of the occupant which turns out to be a near-black, nicely put-together gelding.

"He's a horse!" I say to Violet.

My niece nods. "When Patrick took over Milford, Mom and Dad decided I needed something big enough to last me for a while."

"He's lovely," I say.

"Violet can't ride him," Ali says.

"I can."

"Can't."

"Of course I can."

"Not very well."

"At least I *try*."

"Girls!" It's just as well the admonition comes from the teenager in the doorway — Marta, I presume — instead of me. Marta's voice is warm, with a little lift in it that says, *Stop being silly and let's sort all this out.* I was on the verge of saying, "Oh, shut up!"

"You should be halfway tacked up by now," Marta says. She flicks a long fishtail braid over her shoulder. "Come on, I'll help."

There are no more horses in the barn, and nobody's mentioned Quinte yet, and with all my recent nostalgia attacks, I'm really not sure how I'll react to seeing him, so I grab a jelly scrubber and get to work on Violet's new gelding.

***

Marta isn't a very good riding instructor. She has a sweet upturn to the corners of her mouth, a musical voice, and a laugh like a small, friendly waterfall. She also knows how to turn a horse out — Milford, Cressy, and Banks all gleam in the sun, and the two who are tacked up wear lovely even saddle pads and carefully snugged girths.

But, *teach* — that she can't do.

Within two minutes flat I've figured out that Milford is a complete pushbutton, and that Cressy likely would be, too, if Ali would do more than lead her around the outside of the sand ring.

Marta's fine with those two. "Bring Milford over these trot poles," she tells Patrick. Then, as Milford pricks his sweet ears forward and strides straight down the middle of the poles, she claps, "Great job Patrick! Give him a pat!"

She even offers guidance to Ali. "Make sure she walks by your shoulder. She needs to halt when you stop."

Cressy walks politely next to Ali, seemingly just as happy to be schooled on the ground as from the saddle.

Then there's Banks. He's — well — he's those words people use when they want to let you know what kind of horse, or person, you're dealing with but they don't want to come right out and say it.

He's sensitive.

He's challenging.

If Marta wasn't such a perfect tacker-upper, I'd swear she left a burr under his saddle pad.

Violet has a heck of a time mounting. Girl and horse do an endless shuffling dance around the mounting block until finally he's fairly close for a couple of seconds and she scrambles into the saddle.

There's already a glimmer of tears in her eyes, and the second she settles into the saddle, the horse scoots forward.

"Shorten your reins," Marta says.

Violet does, and Banks begins mincing. He might not technically be trotting but he's definitely not walking. Violet lets out a ragged breath as the horse snorts his way past me.

"Give him a half-halt," Marta instructs. It's not the world's worst advice except, as so many riders do, Violet neglects the "half" part of the halt. She takes, without releasing. Banks responds to this new restriction by bouncing into a trot.

"Take your leg off!" Marta calls, and that's it. I can't stay quiet any longer. I can't let my niece be ruined as a rider, and her horse be spoiled because Marta clearly has no idea how to teach on anything other than Patrick and Ali's trained-to-the-eyeballs ponies, or schooling horses who've had most of their will to live ridden out of them.

"Stop!"

Milford and Cressy snap into perfect, square halts. Patrick, Ali, and Marta stare at me. Violet takes a stronger hold on the reins. Banks deepens the bow in his neck and launches into a canter and Violet wails, "I can't, Auntie Hazel!"

Oh, for goodness' sake ...

I step into the ring. I look down at my leggings and running shoes. They'll have to do.

The horse knows I'm coming. The ear he flicks toward me tells me so. The fact that he's acknowledging me is a good sign. He's not wild. He's not out of control. He's just sensitive, and he doesn't like the way he's being ridden.

I don't blame him.

"Look at me, Violet," I say.

"But ..."

"Just look at me."

I stand still, hold my hand out, and — sure enough — the horse bounces to an agitated stop in front of me, nostrils flaring, breath huffing, with his chin nearly touching his chest. "It's OK." I'm saying it to him, and to my niece. "You're fine." And they both are — physically — although no thanks to whoever put a mild-mannered inexperienced rider on this hot horse, then tied him down with far too much equipment.

I reach out and loosen his much-too-tight noseband. "Auntie Hazel …" Violet protests.

"Don't worry, honey. You just scratch his withers and tell him he's a good boy, then dismount."

I don't have to ask her twice. In a second she's standing behind me. "I can't ride him."

"I think you can, but I think you both need a break." As I'm talking to her, I'm unbuckling his reins, removing the running martingale restricting his head.

"He's too wild."

Fortunately the martingale is attached to his girth with a snap on a d-ring. I undo it. "Is it OK with you if I ride him and show you how I think he can go for you?"

She takes a deep breath and I feel something nudging my ribs. It's her helmet, held out to me. "OK, then. Let's see how this goes."

I don't start by riding him.

I lead him around the ring until he stops jigging and starts walking. Until he willingly lines his shoulder up with mine and matches my pace. Until we've gone the whole way round once without him snorting, or slamming into my side, or dancing away.

Then I take him to the mounting block and before he has time to think about it, or get worked up, I put my leg over his back. He takes a step forward and I immediately say, "Hep! No," and holding the reins firmly I apply my legs until he takes a step back. I scratch his withers. "Good."

He swings forward into an energetic walk and, instead of trying to slow him, I leave my reins long and let my hips follow the rhythm of his stride.

When I ask him to trot, I'm ready for the surge that comes with the transition. He's ready, too. For the yank that comes as he accelerates. For the resistance he can pull against.

I don't give him any. I just set my reins at a very generous length and — the opposite of Marta's advice — put my leg on. His confusion is clear in the rapid swiveling of his ears and the inconsistency of his pace. He scoots for a few strides, then backs off, then rushes forward again.

I scratch his withers again — "settle" — and start taking him through a series of circles, twists, and turns. Every time he tries to speed up, I ask him to bend. Because he can't bend and bolt at the same time, I'm able to keep him from running without restricting him.

Because I'm not restricting him, he doesn't try to run away.

Patrick's riding Milford again, and Ali's leading Cressy. Banks and I circle around them a few times, then I say, "Walk," and drop my weight into my seat and heels, and he walks. I let the reins out to the buckle and he lowers his head and stretches it out. I ride him to the centre of the ring and slide off his back.

Violet's smiling and it warms my heart. First step accomplished — make her believe the horse can be ridden.

Until Marta speaks up. "It's all fine for you to do that. Violet's never going to be able to."

My heart instantly hardens and takes a backseat to my tongue. "Clearly not if you keep trying to teach her. You're fired."

She gasps. "You can't!"

"I just did."

"You're not my boss!"

"And you're no riding instructor."

Violet looks almost as miserable as when she got off Banks. Patrick and Ali have stopped again and are staring again.

"What, exactly is going on here?" Everyone stops staring at Marta and me, and turns to face my sister-in-law.

***

"Can I talk to you?" Aggie walks away from the ring, back along the drive to the shade of a spreading oak. "You can't be firing our riding instructor."

I make a choking noise.

"What?"

"It's a stretch to call her a riding instructor. More like an equestrian-adjacent babysitter."

Aggie has to know what I mean. Even though I'd rather have a one-on-one sit-down dinner with my mother than admit it, Aggie is — or at least was — a decent rider. Possibly even better than me, when it comes to equitation, but I'd also stay for dessert with my mother rather than tell anyone that.

Still. Both Aggie and I know she knows a good riding instructor when she sees one, and both Aggie and I know Marta is not a good riding instructor.

Aggie sighs. "She's *our* equestrian-adjacent babysitter, who we hired, and who we pay, and the kids like her, and we bought them nice-enough ponies that she just needs to keep them safe."

"Except Banks."

"Banks is a great horse."

"Banks is a great mover. Banks is gorgeous. Banks is smart. I'm betting Banks can jump the moon. Banks is not the horse you'd ever choose for a somewhat-unsureof-herself tween girl making her first move up from a bombproof pony. So, what happened there?"

Aggie makes that face I remember from high school when we were both in Model UN and I — Great Britain — struck a trade deal with the US to completely freeze out France — Aggie.

I was a bitch to her then, and I'm being a bitch to her now.

I know that.

Nine out of ten people — no ... more like ninety-nine out of a hundred — would say Aggie's right and I'm wrong.

I don't dispute that.

I should be trying to be a nicer person.

That's true.

But it's so hard.

And it's especially hard to be nice to Aggie who everybody thinks is so sweet, but who's been feeding micro-insults to my nieces and nephew. It makes me enjoy her discomfort. In fact, I'm opening my mouth to prod her further when Violet calls, "Auntie Hazel!" and I turn around and fix my eyes on a face I haven't seen for years.

Quin.

My stomach twists and my breath hitches. *There's* my guilt. I can't produce it for a human being — for my own sister-in-law — but one look at my old horse and my knees go weak with shame.

Those big dark eyes. Those forward-pricked ears. That blaze that widens as it spills down his face until it turns his entire muzzle white.

He's standing politely by Violet — Quin has never been anything but polite — but as I step forward, he does too, until his face is pressed against my front and my arms are wrapped around his broad cheeks.

Oh lord, I think as his warm breath whiffles through the thin fabric of my leggings, *this is not going to help with my nostalgia problem.*

Four

I DO KNOW I have to see my mother.

Actually, my therapist would probably point out, no, I don't have to. I have to eat, and sleep, and breathe. I'm not *required* to see my mother.

Except by her.

Lest you think this requirement is because she loves me, and would already have been on the doorstep of the trailer with open arms and home cooking if she knew I was here, let me explain that's not it at all.

The fact is, my mother will feel slighted when she discovers I came without telling her, and that my brother knows something she doesn't.

If any of her friends in town discover that I'm here before she does, her ego will never stand it. There will be tears and the unanswerable questions — "What did I ever do to deserve being treated like this?" and "Do you care so little for my feelings?"

Because even I'm not blunt enough to answer those questions honestly, the path of least resistance is to forestall them by going to see her.

This is what I'm thinking about as I sit on the front porch of the farmhouse, cupping my morning mug of coffee and waiting for the sounds of the blender, and the microwave, and voices rising and falling to abate — for the morning kitchen rush hour to be over — so I can nip back inside and help myself to some of Aggie's really-quite-delicious homemade granola.

There's a new message on my phone from Tom. I haven't opened it and don't want to considering the first five words I can see are, **You are the most selfish.**

Nobody needs to start their day by reading a message like that.

Besides, Tom's never met my mother.

Back to her ... I'm cut off mid-sigh by the same-as-it-ever-was creak of the screen door. "Hey, Aunt Hazel."

Violet sinks to the step next to me. She's holding a mug that matches mine, with steam wisping out the top. As I watch she glances sideways, then rearranges her hands to cup her drink in the same way I am.

It's nice that I have one fan in this world.

"How's my favourite almost-teenage niece?"

"I'm good, but I'm your only almost-teenage ... oh, it was a joke."

While living on the West Coast I did a pretty good job of training myself not to feel guilt. But between thinking about my mother and disappointing my niece, it's staging a quick comeback. "Well, more of an inside joke — between you and me."

She nods. "OK. I get it. So ..."

"So, what?"

"So, if it's OK to talk about things between just you and me, can we talk about Ali?"

"Sure. What about Ali?"

"You understand about her?"

Oh my. I wonder if Violet even realizes how big her question is. My brain's racing to decide which level of "understanding" we're even talking about here and a silence is developing where I really don't want there to be any silence.

"I love Ali. I love all of you, exactly as you are." *Although, a little less attitude from Patrick would be nice ...*

"Phew!" She takes a sip of her drink and her eyes open wide. Too hot, I'm guessing.

While she's recovering, I ask, "Why do you say 'phew?'"

She forms an "O" with her mouth — probably to blow air across her burnt tongue. "I heard Mom and Dad talking. They said 'We'll have to see how Hazel takes it — she has strong opinions.'"

OK. I've had it. Everyone else might think Aggie's an angel, but I know the truth. I'm going to go straight in there and — as soon as I fill my bowl with granola — tell her what I think about all these innuendos.

Except, Violet's still talking. I regain my focus in time to hear her say, "... tired of people with strong opinions. I had to beat a few people up this year, and even though things should be equal between boys and girls, it's still mostly harder for a girl to beat up a boy."

"Wait a minute — are you saying you had to beat people up because of Ali?"

Violet nods. "Because of what they said about her."

"I ..." Once again I'm at a loss for words as my brain races through the layers and levels of what she's just told me.

"Yes, Auntie Hazel?"

I add this to my list of things to discuss with my sister-in-law, and say, "If you think anyone needs beating up, tell me, OK?"

She shrugs. "OK, but it mostly happens during school." Then she smiles. "It's nice of you to say it, though."

Which brings a swift return of the guilt — saying but not doing is a classic move of my mom and more than I don't want to see her today, I definitely don't want to turn into her.

***

"Your brother tells me the wedding is off."

Turns out I wasn't quick enough. My brother came by to mow my mother's lawn this morning sometime while I was eating Aggie's granola.

So, he's ahead of me on two counts 1) performing menial labour for my mother, 2) being the first to inform her of significant news / gossip.

Whatever. I was never going to win with her.

I stifle my sigh and nod. "He's right."

"I already bought my dress."

I think: *Of course it's about you.* I say: "I'll take you out for dinner so you can wear it."

"There's no place around here to wear a dress like this. I took the train to Toronto to buy it from Karolina Magdalena."

"I'm sorry, am I supposed to know her?"

"It's not a 'her,' they're sisters. They designed the dresses for the Carmichael wedding."

I don't know what the Carmichael wedding is, but clearly I'm supposed to be impressed. I start, "OK ..." but my mom cuts me off.

"It's a huge disappointment."

"That I don't know who Karolina Magdalena is?" My mom shoots me a laser glance. "*Are?*"

"That you're not getting married after all. It was always a good distraction in Book Club when Harriet would start talking about her son, George, and his never-ending voyage through medical school. The last time I shut her down by telling her you'd ordered your wedding cake from an appointment-only bakery and it cost more than the car George bought from his neighbour which promptly broke down."

"But, I didn't ..."

My mom waves her hand. "You always did expect too much."

"Excuse me?"

"I thought you'd gotten all your silly romantic notions out of your head. Thought you'd finally listened to me — it's just as easy to marry a rich man as a poor one and, while it's true you could do better than that fiancé of yours, it does sound like he'll make a decent salary before long. He's good-looking as well, so I'm not sure what more you think you deserve."

As much as I hate to admit it, her words hurt.

My mother isn't the kind of woman who inspires nostalgia. In fact she'd hate it if I suggested it — she was never a fan of living on the farm and "the old days were not the good days" is something she's said many times.

This snug new bungalow in the village isn't one I've ever lived in.

In theory, then, it should be easy for me to hold on to my West-Coast-hardened persona. My I-don't-give-a-damn mindset.

But it seems like my old horse, and my young nieces and nephew, and the smells, and sights, and sounds of the farm are in danger of wearing my edges down.

The phone rings and my presence doesn't even make my mom hesitate. She lifts the receiver to her ear and injects smoke rings into her voice. "Hel-lo ... oh Bruce, how lovely," she purrs.

Bruce is her boyfriend — if you can call a seventy-year-old a boyfriend. He's the mayor of the county, owns and flies his own small plane, and picks my mom up for dinner-and-theatre outings in his Cadillac.

As far as I can tell, he's a perfectly nice man — much too nice for my mother — but, as always, listening to my mom talk to any man who admires her is enough to trigger a sugar rush.

"I'll let myself out," I say.

She furrows her brow and places a finger across her lips, mouthing a silent *shush*.

I resist the urge to slam the door behind me as I step out onto the porch.

As I'm walking down the steps, a car pulls up. A truck, actually. A very familiar truck.

Aggie.

Super-fantastic. I believe this is the textbook definition of adding insult to injury.

Aggie reaches into the back of the truck and pulls out a laundry basket which she carries up the path. "Hey."

"Hey."

She glances down at the basket, then up at me. "I'm bringing her laundry back." Lawn-mowing and laundry. I don't stand a chance against Aggie and Brody's domestic services.

"She's on the phone with Bruce."

Aggie laughs. It's sudden, and it's like the sun coming out. "That's actually perfect. She won't want to talk to me."

Aggie's right. She's back outside without the basket faster than I can gather myself to return to my little car which still has the air of being ridden hard and put away wet.

"It's nice of you to do her laundry." I make a half-hearted attempt to keep my tone neutral.

Aggie's tone isn't neutral at all when she answers, "She doesn't think so. I don't iron her sheets."

Ironed sheets ... ironed jeans, for that matter ... polished silver, the kitchen sink buffed twice daily, no dishes allowed to be left out to air-dry, fresh flowers on the hall table at all times, nothing left on bedroom floors, ever — all the rigid rules of daily life with my mother come flooding back; rules that were even more crazy back when we lived in a century farmhouse surrounded by livestock, and my dad worked the land, and my brother and I were kids, running in and out.

I've still only ventured into the farmhouse as far as the kitchen, but already I have to admit Aggie's basically-clean-but-more-relaxed housekeeping style is far more to my liking than when I grew up there.

I should tell her.

That feels too hard, but I manage a smile.

When she reciprocates with a grin, the warmth that floods me catches me off guard. It also infuses me with spontaneity and generosity. I think of the café on main street that's always served my favourite quesadilla, where I haven't eaten for years. "Do you want to get lunch?"

Aggie's smile retreats. Her eyes flick away from mine. The warmth leaves me. "Fine. Whatever."

"It's not that," my sister-in-law says.

"What is it then?"

"We just found out Violet needs braces. It's hard to justify eating lunch out when we have groceries at home."

I don't care what groceries Aggie has — she can't make a quesadilla to rival the one at the café. "It's my vacation — I'm paying."

* * *

We sit at the prime table at the back corner of the outside deck by the creek. I've already seen a quesadilla being carried to another table and it looks exactly the way

I remember it. The sun's just a bit too bright so I've asked for an umbrella and the waiter's carrying it over now.

He slots it into place — "Lucky you, this was the last one we had" — and promises to be back with our drinks. Aggie looks at the rushing creek, then at me. "I've never sat here in all my years in the County."

"This is the best table, bar none."

"That's my point. You get whatever you want. The best table. The last umbrella."

A called-off engagement. A deep questioning of where I belong in life. A sister-in-law who talks about me behind my back. Which reminds me, I was going to call her on that.

Before I can, though, she presses on. "I just don't know how you do it ..."

"I'm surprised, because you seem to know everything about me. Or, at least, you seem to think you do."

"What do you mean?" Her voice is rising. I'm about to snap back any one of the many things my nieces and nephews have passed onto me. But ... I don't want to dump them in it.

Instead I choose one I heard firsthand. "Well, for example, I wasn't being flip about Tom, you know. I really did make my final decision on the drive here, and considering that drive was 4500 kilometres long, I had a lot of time to think about it."

Aggie looks down, fiddles with her napkin, rearranges her cutlery and I wonder if that's it — if I've lost her. I hope not. I don't want to have to leave this perfect table, with its miracle umbrella, and I don't want to take my quesadilla back to the trailer in a styrofoam container.

"I'm supposed to apologize to you."

"Excuse me?" I'm not, actually, being a bitch. Not trying to make her repeat her apology. It's just that I think she said something about apologizing and I find that really hard to believe.

"Brody says I always think the worst of you."

Unfortunately, as an apology I'd have to give it a failing grade considering all it does is confirm that she complains about me to other people. "You do? That's good to know."

She sighs. "Not the worst. I shouldn't have said that. But, I mean, I just remember how you were in school. Always sure you were right. You weren't exactly popular, because you didn't care enough to bother with that, but everyone knew you. Everyone listened to you. That head girl speech ..." She shakes her head.

It was a long time ago, but I know exactly what she means. I won head girl that year and, unlike the two girls who ran against me on campaigns of more dances and extra colour pages in the yearbook, I told the student body they needed a strong representative and that the other candidates wouldn't get anything done. "They might seem nice, but they're actually weak. Amanda froze on the last word in the County spelling bee and Portia let East High beat us in the girls' soccer final last year." East High was our arch rival. "East has our soccer trophy!" I declared into the mike. "Do you want a loser as your head girl?"

So, yes, definitely not nice. But effective. And something the others could have done for themselves as well. It's not my fault they chose not to.

I've never cheated, or stolen, or broken rules or laws, but I've always been willing to do anything within them to get what I need and that's why I've been able to afford to live in one of the world's most expensive cities. It's why I was on track to marry an already-making-good-money-and-destined-to-earn-much-more guy. I was doing fine with my do-what-I-need-to philosophy.

Until I saw my future and it looked like the woman I've just left behind in the soulless bungalow.

I tune back in, in time to register Aggie saying, "That wasn't the best apology."

"Since it didn't actually contain the word 'sorry' I'd argue it wasn't an apology at all."

Aggie rubs her forehead. "OK. I'm sorry. Will that do?"

The waiter arrives holding my quesadilla and my stomach gives a very big rumble. "I want to eat, so I guess it'll have to."

***

There's still lots of light left, but it's much softer than it was earlier, as is the air. I lean on the fence and gaze across the turn-out field. The grassy area is empty right now — the horses and ponies must be in the cool of the trees — but my senses are full anyway with the buzzing of bees on a nearby patch of bee balm and the incessant trilling of insects, and birds, and frogs.

Earlier, my brain was full too — whirling, actually — with thoughts of the fiancé, and job, and life I left behind. With questions of how smart it was to flee to a place where my sister-in-law has to make an effort to tolerate me and any amount of time spent with my mother makes my stomach ache.

Which is why, when Violet knocked on the trailer door and asked if I'd like to join the family at a neighbour's barbecue, I'd said no thank you.

I've been walking the farm ever since. Thinking, even though I grew up here, it's one of the only times I've ever had the whole place to myself. Distracting myself by throwing sticks for the neighbour's dog who seems to spend a lot of time here, and feeding the chickens. Following the overgrown lane that leads past the barn to the old sugar shack. It's been a long-time quiet, but there was a period when my dad tapped maples and, for a few weekends every spring horse-drawn sleighs would bring people back along this lane for massive brunches where everything was maple themed and flavoured — the baked beans, the sausages, and of course our own home-boiled maple syrup.

I can picture him — a tall man with big hands, who loved being outside — standing on the now-sagging porch, welcoming each sleigh as it arrived.

My brother would be tending to the big fire that reduced the sap to syrup, and I'd be managing things inside with the paying guests — keeping the ship running as tightly as possible so we'd actually made a profit out of that short-lived season.

Sky-reaching spruce and trembling aspen tower behind the rustic building, and the approach to it is a waist-deep obstacle course of milkweed, tansy, and goldenrod. I remember there being a path here but, then again, we always used it in the winter when the tromped-down snow of hundreds of winter boots made their own track so maybe it was always like this and it's my nostalgic bent gold-tinting my memories.

I wade through the green abundance trying not to think of ticks, and step onto the porch. It starts as a step, anyway, and turns into a twisting hop as there's a suspicious give to the first board I put my weight on.

At least peering through the grimy windows doesn't flare my nostalgia. Unfortunately, the place was always ugly, and that hasn't been improved by time and neglect.

Linoleum floors in murky shades of green and yellow. Wood paneling of the cheap-and-dark, rather than rustic-and-charming variety. And detritus — both human and animal-generated. Although I'm more inclined to forgive the squirrels for building nests in the corners, than to pardon whoever decided this would be a good place to have a few beers and smokes, it all looks terrible.

A glimpse of the classic outline of a maple syrup can sparks some sentimentality. As well as a sudden urge for the incomparable mix of sweet syrup and salty butter melting over fluffy pancakes.

I shake my head and carefully pick my way back off the sagging porch and through the wild vegetation. Because, unlike the pure tooth-aching flavour of the syrup, my memories are bittersweet.

Not only was my mother never in them, but she was increasingly hostile as the years wore on. Wanting to be on the farm less and less. Not just staying separate from the work that happened there, but actively disparaging it. "This farm is less-and-less valuable for the work you can get out of it, and more-and-more valuable for the price of the acreage."

As the County became increasingly popular with Toronto weekend warriors, she became more fixated on severing the farm into large country acreages and selling them off. "The profit would buy us a nice house in town. I never agreed to live here forever."

My dad only ever bit his lip when she said things like that, but when he died, we found out he'd been paying monthly premiums on a significant life insurance policy and had specifically left the farm to Brody and me, and the insurance policy to my mother.

As I return to the field, I'm acutely aware that without my father's foresight all the places I walked by tonight — not just the rustic sugar shack, but also the sweet-and-tiny (and now boarded-up) cabin that was the original house on the land back when my grandparents first bought it, the snug stables, and all the acres and acres of fields and woodlot — they'd all be long sold and probably demolished.

As a late shaft of evening sun falls across my face, I'm glad they're not.

Even if I've left my brother entirely on his own when it comes to running this place.

I thought I could just walk away, but it seems I was wrong.

As if on cue, to remind me of things I can't just walk away from, several shadowy shapes emerge from the trees.

As they reach the open area, the sun picks out Milford's reddish tints, and Cressy's dapples, and makes Bank's coat gleam, but the one I'm really looking for — the one who makes my heart break with the complicated combination of loving him and having left him — is the handsome bay who steadily, quietly, and unwaveringly steps his way to me and shoves his muzzle into my hand.

Five

IT'S QUITE DEPRESSING when I scroll through my messages and realize they're all about subjects I'm trying to ignore and none of them at all are giving me joy.

That's not true — there's *one* nice one, from my next-door neighbour, Paisley, at the condo. We were roommates at university. We were rarely home at the same time, but when we were, we'd always make each other laugh. It seemed like a good reason to buy side-by-side condos once we both got real jobs and now, whenever either of us is away we water each other's plants, and collect each other's mail. It's an equal relationship, based on mutual respect and, now that I think about it, probably the most functional (*only* functional?) one in my life.

At first I laugh, because she's sent a photo of the mail room, where one of our fellow condo-mates constructs elaborate assembled sculptures out of Amazon packages. Today's appears to be some form of poultry. **Chicken or rooster?** I'm about to text, when I read the rest of Paisley's message.

Finally convinced my boss we need to have a presence at Down-Under Days and ... wait for it ... I. Am. The. One. Going.

There's a link that confirms my worst fears. The conference — halfway around the world — starts soon. Much sooner than I was anticipating returning to Vancouver. *My plants, my mail* ... wow, my mom would be proud of how well she's succeeded in programming me to take my friend's success and make it all about me.

I wrinkle my nose, bite my lip, and text back, **Persistence Paisley wins again — your boss didn't stand a chance. And I see this year the conference is in the Gold Coast. Amazing!**

Shit. Or sugar. Or whatever Aggie wants me to say. I have a spider plant I've kept alive for a whole year. Who's going to water it now?

I scan the rest of my messages. Tom hasn't sent any fresh notes, but all his previous, quite nasty ones are still there, and there's a fresh one from work. **So, are you feeling any better, yet?** I'd like to think they're asking in a supportive way, but I know they're not.

Clearly both my ex-fiancé and my colleagues are out as plant-sitters. I doubt Chantal would agree after hairpiece-gate.

Worry about it later. I try. I go on a really long run. I find a bucket and sponge in Brody's tractor shed and have a go at resurrecting the cuteness of my little car. I go grocery shopping and buy way more than I could ever eat.

Still, by mid-afternoon I'm sitting on the metal steps of the trailer, chin in hand, staring at my newly sparkling hatchback wondering if I should just get back in it and retrace my 4,500 kilometres.

At least work would be happy I was back.

Or, less pissed off that I was missing.

That's when I hear high-pitched voices, and running footsteps, and the children scamper up the gravel drive yelling, "Auntie Hazel! Auntie Hazel! We need help!"

Violet and Ali jump around me, eyes shining. "On the last day of school we had so many things to carry home that we left most of them in the bus shelter. Now Mom says we have to clear it out before the festival. We can't carry everything!" Sure enough, they're both dropping notebooks, and trying to hold on to miscellaneous items like a single rain boot, a Yo-Yo, a Rubik's Cube.

Patrick hangs back, head tilted, squinting at me through one eye.

"Girls! Girls! I'll help you! Here ..." I duck back into the trailer and grab a copious tote bag. I plunk it on the ground in front of them. "Put the things you can't carry in this and I'll carry it for you."

Then I turn to Patrick. I already have my mother and Aggie to struggle with. I don't want this nine-year-old to be against me as well. "I have something for you."

He does the one-eyebrow-lift thing. The message comes across clear as day. *It had better be good. ...*

One more trip back into the trailer's kitchenette and I return holding a box. Patrick's eyes widen.

I proffer it to Patrick. An entire box — family-sized — of Lucky Charms. "For you."

"Really?"

I nod.

"All of it?"

"Nobody else is allowed to open it."

Like his sisters, his arms are full of school paraphernalia. "Can I put some things in your tote bag?"

"Of course you can."

One enemy down. Let's not count how many to go.

At the house, we don't even go inside. The kids dump their accumulation of school detritus on the front porch and yell, "Come on! To the pond!"

I have no idea what's going on, but I also don't have anything better to do, so I follow them to the pond.

This is one spot I didn't visit on my evening wander last night. Mostly because it never occurred to me to do so. When I was growing up, this section of the farm was the LVP – the Least Valuable Parcel. The swarming mosquitos reminded us there was some kind of wet depression / wetland / basin in the middle of a tangle of growth and that was exactly why we never came here.

From my dad's perspective it was an area where he couldn't plant anything. From my mom's perspective the overgrowth surrounding it was bound to be filled with even more mice, and voles, and snakes than the rest of the farm.

From the perspective of me and my brother, growing up as we did on a chunk of land surrounded by Lake Ontario and liberally dotted with various charming inland lakes, this puddle on our land wasn't worthy of any attention.

I can see that's all changed.

As I follow my nieces and nephew through a natural arch created by several exuberantly overgrown cedars, I emerge onto a scene that can only be described as charming. Possibly magical. Definitely inviting.

What used to be a snarl of vegetation is now a hayfield with the still-early grasses already growing long enough to wave in the breeze. Trees line the field on all four sides, so even though it's huge, it feels cosy.

There's a worn dirt path which the kids have already pounded along. It's about fifty metres long, and it leads to an expansive wooden platform which I'm not sure whether to call a deck or a dock. There are brightly coloured Muskoka chairs scattered around, and the far end is built out over the edge of the pond which I think surely can't be the pond of my childhood because the water winks in the sunlight and there's a cluster of sturdy plastic kayaks tied to one post and one of those indestructible pedal boats tied to another.

A gust of air ruffles the water's surface and carries the summer smell to me and I'm seized with that feeling again — the one that started all the problems back in Vancouver — I know if I kick off my sandals the wood will be warm under my feet, and if I run and jump in, the water will be cool … and fresh this time. No salt water.

Before the temptation can become too great, a racket of stomping feet and arguing children, all holding freezies, snaps my attention to my left. "What flavour is white? I always forget," "It's cream soda and it's yucky!" "No, the blue is yucky," "The blue is raspberry!" "Raspberries aren't blue …"

I look past them to Aggie standing on the porch of a rustic barnboard structure. Her hands rest on the wood railing, and the expression on her face as she watches her children scamper away gives me a nostalgia rush of a different sort. It's the longing-for-what-never-was variety of wistfulness. My mother never looked at me that way.

In addition to my devoted sister-in-law, I also take in the strings of vintage Edison lightbulbs outlining the windows and door, and what must be a commercial-grade barbecue. Cases of beer and soft drinks are stacked on the floor.

"Is all this for me?" I ask. "You really shouldn't have."

Aggie pulls her attention away from the kids — all three of whom have now climbed onto a tire swing strung from one of the trees near the start of the path. "You laugh, but your mother will be here soon in her bathing suit and heels, and she'll expect to have a chilled martini waiting for her."

I watch as Patrick hangs out one side of the tire, Ali the other, and Violet spins them both. "Speaking of the grande dame, what did she say about Ali?"

Aggie reaches behind her, then steps off the porch and carries two drinks over, dripping with cold condensation in the strong sun. "Sorry. Just soda for now. I can't drink alcohol this early."

I push two chairs into place facing the tire swing. "Fine with me."

We sit and Aggie sighs. "So. Your mother. The problem with her is she knows what she's not supposed to say. It's almost easier to deal with people who are straight-up ignorant, or rude." She shakes her head. "She's very publicly supportive, and I think she's told everyone in the village at least twice how understanding she is, then ..." She lifts her hands.

"Drip-drip-drip?" I suggest.

"That's it!" Aggie says. "Whenever she gets me alone it's 'Have you gotten proper advice?' 'Are you taking her to a therapist?' 'Is the therapist qualified?' 'Did she get this idea from social media?'"

"The not-innocent-at-all-innocent questions." I shudder. "I know them well."

Aggie shoots me a sideways glance and I can almost see her thinking, *oh, yeah?*

I watch my younger niece — head thrown back, long hair flying through the air, along with the blue freezie clamped in her mouth — and the urge to show my solidarity breaks down my normal reticence to share with my sister-in-law. "You know how we used to go to Kingston for track meets in high school?"

Aggie pulls her brows together, like *What do track meets have to do with anything* ... "I know *you* did."

It's tempting to get sidetracked into one of our many familiar old argumentative rabbit-holes:

- "Just because you didn't make the team."

- "More like, 'Just because I wouldn't be a member of any team alongside Brent Jackson."

- "It was an athletic contest, not a personality test."

- "Being a racist pig isn't personality, and you can compartmentalize morals ..."

Usually these rote debates are the only way I know how to relate to, or communicate with Aggie.

But I'm surprised how much I want to have this conversation with her.

I lift my hand. "I know you never much liked the people who ran track and, to be honest, neither did I, which is why the one time we had an overnight there, they all snuck into the university pub but I stayed back at the hotel ..."

Oh god. Why did I start this? I take a deep breath. "The track organization had a conference room there, where they kept all the numbers and swag bags, and there was this guy, sorting them all out. He was young and funny and everyone knew him. I ended up helping him. He told me if there was leftover swag at the end, I could keep it."

Aggie still looks puzzled, but she nods.

"At one point he told me there were two extra boxes of stuff in his room. I went with him to get them. I didn't even think about it."

Aggie makes a tiny noise. Like she knows what's coming. It's almost because of that noise — to keep her from making another one — that I keep going.

"The door closed behind us — of course it did — I mean, hotel doors, do. I asked him where the boxes were and he said, 'Don't worry about boxes,' and ... it wasn't ... I mean ... it could have been much worse ... he wasn't physical, but he got so angry, so quickly. He yelled at me that I was a bitch and a cock-tease. He told me to get out and I wanted to, badly, but I had to walk past him — you know in that narrow part of a hotel room by the bathroom? — I was shaking. I thought my knees would give way, or I'd throw up. It took me three tries to get the door open, and I kept thinking he'd grab me from behind. And when I got into the hall there was a woman, with her door open. She asked if everything was OK, and that's how I knew I hadn't imagined how loudly he'd yelled."

I pause, then look right in Aggie's eyes. "And later, back at home, I made the mistake of telling my mother, and she said, 'Have you thought about what you might have done to bring that on yourself?' So, micro-aggressive questions from my mother? Yes, I know about them."

"Hazel ..." Aggie reaches over and puts her hand on my arm. "That's terrible."

I shrug. "That's my mother."

"No, really. That's awful. I'm sorry that happened to you."

For the last ten days or so I've been feeling little twinges of emotion. Flutters in my stomach, tightness in my chest. When Aggie says that, though, I feel something different — bigger, stronger. I feel something breaking away and disintegrating inside me. I feel the warmth of the sun more strongly on my skin and the weight of my body in the chair.

"I'm sorry you have to deal with my mother's input about Ali," I reply.

Just as Aggie and I are in danger of slipping into a mutual-support therapy session, we're interrupted by a man's voice, "OK! I'm done!"

"Oh! Gus! Thanks!" Aggie springs out of her chair in one smooth motion which, to be honest, is not all that easy to do from the low-slung Muskoka chairs. There's a hint of breathlessness in my normally self-contained sister-in-law's voice and from my spot behind her I can see her fiddling with her ponytail.

I lever myself out of my chair in a more slo-mo fashion only to face the cause of Aggie's agitation.

Oh, come on.

Really?

A man, shirtless and barefoot, with water dripping from the hems of his soaking wet jeans.

Everything about this situation is surprising. I'm not sure why a man who looks like he's been styled for the cover of a romance novel is on the deck at my family farm. I'm not sure why the unflappable Aggie seems to have lost the ability to string more than two words together. I'm not entirely sure why it all makes me want to burst out laughing, but unfortunately, it does.

"Why ..." Aggie starts. "I mean, you're wet ..." Stating the obvious. "I didn't expect ..." I giggle a little more with each of Aggie's stutter-stop-and-starts, until the guy looks at me and says, "Am I missing something?"

Now I'm the one stuttering as the laughter seizes me firmly in its grip. "It's just ... you standing there ... and there's pondweed stuck on your belt loop ... and a leech on your toe ..."

"What!" He does a funny jump-dance step. As though that's going to dislodge a leech.

He spins around, which of course still isn't going to shake off any self-respecting leech, but is definitely adding to my mirth.

I could totally and absolutely pull that leech off. It's not something that freaks me out. But I'm so weak from laughing I have zero fine motor control.

Fortunately the kids show up to save the day. "Hi Mom! Hi Gus! Hi Auntie Hazel! Why are you laughing so hard, Auntie Hazel?"

I point at the toe with the leech on it and gasp, "Leech! Toe!"

"Oh!" Ali darts forward, squats on her haunches and does a quick grab, then a flick, and stands back up. "Leech gone!" Then all three of them thump off the deck yelling, "Bye Mom! Bye Gus! Bye Auntie Hazel!"

I finally manage to take a deep breath, and place one hand over my now-aching stomach while holding out the other. "I'm guessing you must be Gus."

***

"Thanks." Until now, Aggie's been silently handing me items — plates, cutlery, food — accompanied only by very short, extremely terse orders. "Set up the trestle table and put these on it," "Tell Brody we'll need more sausages."

It was on the trip to Brody — who I talked to through the shower curtain while he washed away the dust and sweat of a day spent in the fields — that I found out what was going on.

"It's our TGIF barbecue," he called over the splash of the water and the hum of the fan. "We have them every Friday from the summer solstice to the autumn equinox. Our friends will start showing up in a bit, which is why I need a little privacy to get out and dry off if you don't mind."

"I'm not sure why you didn't just jump in the pond ..." I mumbled, with a surprisingly vivid image of Gus in my head.

"Excuse me?"

"Nothing! Just remember the sausages!" I yelled as I pulled the bathroom door shut behind me.

I've just returned from that mission when Aggie spits out her "Thanks," presumably in response to me splitting open a case of Diet Coke, but no Diet Coke should ever prompt a tone that acrimonious.

"Oh, we're speaking now?"

"Correct. I'm speaking. Not falling down laughing."

"Oh. So that's what this is about ... and, for the record, I didn't fall down."

"You might as well have," she says.

"Why do you care?"

"Because he's a nice person, OK? Because he's helping us with repairs that really need to get done. Because he went into the pond, in his jeans, to check out the underside of the dock and make sure it's safe for twenty-five people to be on it tonight."

"Hmm ... yes, the going-into-the-pond-in-his-jeans part was hard to miss." I pause in my work twisting cans into the cooler full of ice to waggle my eyebrows at her.

"You. Are. So. Infuriating."

I shrug. "I'm sure I am. All you have to do is tell him I'm your annoying sister-in-law from Vancouver. He looks like a good old boy so he'll assume I'm an almond-milk-drinking, Green-party-voting vegan and he'll feel sorry for you for having to deal with me, and he won't hold my behaviour against you."

"Oh," Aggie says, "Don't worry. I've already done that. Also ..." She points into the now-full cooler, "I'm not really sure we need twenty-four Diet Cokes in the cooler and nothing else."

As she walks away, I mutter, "Fine, why don't I find some Bud and stick it in there to make the shirtless crowd happy?"

***

The evening's turning out to be quite nice.

Mostly because my brother grills a mean burger, and someone brought squares I remember from my childhood — multi-coloured mini-marshmallows bound together with peanut butter. Heaven.

Also because I've managed to completely avoid Aggie and my mother (who, yes, did show up in sandals with perilously high heels wearing a flowy cover-up over a bikini) and I've spent most of my time so far pushing a gaggle of kids on the tire swing.

As the sky darkens, and the air cools, someone lights a fire in the pit near the edge of the deck. The kids cluster around, like moths to the flames, and Aggie hands out roasting sticks and gives Violet a bag of marshmallows — "Only give them one at a time," her mom warns her.

I lean against the edge of the deck and let the sights, sounds, and feelings of the night seep in. I'd forgotten about the golden gossamer spray of the stars layered as deeply into the inky sky as the eye can see.

There's the rich smoke of the campfire curling into my nostrils, competing with the crisp fresh smell of the cool creeping up from the earth and in from the water.

There's that feeling, again, in the pit of my stomach. The one I've had whenever I rest for a moment lately.

The one that's prompted me to keep driving, running, grocery shopping, anything so I don't have to sit with it for too long.

The one that, now I am sitting with it, I can't even tell if it comes from happiness or sadness. I'm pretty sure it's a swirl of both — battling it out — sometimes one surfaces, sometimes it's the other.

I think I'm on the verge of having a deep thought about how I might need to be prepared to feel the bad, to truly appreciate the good, when my mother's voice cuts into my serenity.

It's a gift she has.

"Of course Brody never was a financial wizard, and it's not like he picked the right wife to help him with that."

"Oh, goodness ..." I recognize the voice as one of the neighbours from down the road who lived here when I was growing up. Mrs. Rose. I thought she was about a hundred when I was a kid, but somehow she still looks the same. When I was a kid I also thought she must have been a perfect mother to her family. There was always a tin full of home-baked cookies in her kitchen and she always called me "dear."

She would never have bad-mouthed her family the way my mother's doing now. "... I've been very supportive of course, even though I do think Aggie could have done more to avoid it ..." Part of me wants to believe she's not talking about Ali, even as most of me knows she is. "It's surprising how well I'm taking it, considering I was told so late in the game. It's easy for my daughter-in-law to come across like the perfectly supportive mother — she's had long enough to get used to it ..."

"You ..." Aggie pushing by me, stepping up onto the deck, confronting my mother. "You poisonous, narrow-minded, hateful ..."

I'm beside her — not as quickly as I'd like to be. My brain was still trying to process what I was hearing when Aggie blew past me, but it *has* processed that emotions are high and I should probably get in there.

I clamp a hand on each of Aggie's arms.

"Oh my goodness." My mother's dabbing at her eyes. It means very little to me as I once overheard her telling my aunt, "If ever somebody attacks me, I always find crying is the best way to get out of it."

Yup. That's my mother.

"Yes, take her away, Hazel," my mother says.

"No way," Aggie's shaking her head. "Don't you dare ..."

I tighten my grip on her arms. "Aggie ..."

She stiffens, wriggles. "She needs to hear this."

"Aggie ..." It's not just her head that's shaking. She's trembling like a leaf. "It's not worth it. She'll never change."

Brody appears. "What's going on?"

"Mom's going home," I tell him. "You should take her."

He holds up a beer. "I can't."

I haven't been drinking but I don't want to let go of Aggie, and I don't want to spend any amount of time alone with my mother in a car.

A man steps forward. "I'm fine to drive. I can take her."

"Thank goodness for that," I mutter. I give Aggie a gentle push and this time she moves. "That's right. Keep walking."

It's only as I'm guiding her back down off the deck that I realize the man who stepped forward to drive my mother home is the formerly streaming wet Gus. I didn't recognize him with a shirt on.

"Come on," I tell Aggie. "Let's round up the kids and I'll help you get them ready for bed."

"You just want to get rid of me."

"No." I shake my head. "That's not it at all."

The truth is, Aggie's not the one I want to get rid of.

Six

IT'S HARD TO FALL ASLEEP. It's hard to stay asleep. I keep running the evening's scenario through my mind. I should have been firmer with my mother. I let Ali down. I let Aggie down.

I do believe what I said to Aggie — and she even agreed with me later, while we were drinking tea in the quiet kitchen — my mom will never change and it's pointless trying to get her to.

Still, every time I'm about to drop off, I think of a zinger I could have laid on my mom. Something I definitely would have said if she was a client.

At some point I do drift off because the light is grey and gritty when I open my eyes with an idea.

Not just an idea. The idea to solve quite a few problems.

Unfortunately, the phone calls I need to make for it to happen are to people back in BC. Where it's 1:15 a.m.

I'd be kidding myself if I thought I could get back to sleep now, so I slide out of bed, and step out into the pearly County light.

A fox trots ahead of me on the path to the barn. He's got his things to think about and I've got mine, so we just coexist.

I pick up a lead rope from the barn and head to the paddock.

When I get to the gate, Quin lifts his white face from the grass, gives a long, rattling exhale, and wanders toward me.

This horse, who I just up and left. Not, as you might think, when I left here for the West Coast — that might be not-ideal, but understandable — no, I actually abandoned him much earlier than that.

When I was a teenager I had a job at a sales barn which I liked because I could ride as much as I wanted, and the horses were never boring. They liked me because they'd never found anything I was afraid of, I could stick on pretty much any horse and make it look good to buyers, and when I did fall, I bounced and got right back up.

I came home one day with dusty breeches and the satisfaction of helping secure the sale of four horses to a riding school in Kingston where they'd be well-treated, and found Quin in the paddock.

"Cramer's selling up," my dad told me, jutting his chin toward a farm up the road. "He's broke — never going to pay me for that hay I sold him. I told him I'd take this guy instead — thought you might like him."

"He's stunning." My dad had grinned then, and I can picture his face just as vividly now, as I run my hand over Quin's ridiculously fine coat, admiring the dapples blooming in it despite living outside with no protection from the sun, and only rare grooming.

Quin was beautiful then, and he's beautiful today. He's a great mover, I can't remember him ever being lame, and he goes English and Western. He's always been sweet and gentle ... and I never enjoyed riding him.

Coming home to ride Quin after being on those sales barn horses was like putting ketchup on your second bowl of mac n' cheese after having hot sauce on your first. The zing just wasn't there.

Aggie, on the other hand, liked her condiments mild, and loved riding Quin.

I finger comb a stray leaf out of his forelock, then straighten it. "Good old, Aggie, hey? Always here for you? Unlike me."

It started with Brody asking if I'd let her ride him. Brody had liked Aggie as long as I'd butted heads with her and I knew he'd been trying to figure out the right angle to ask her out — something different from taking her to the drive-in or the bowling alley where they'd be lined up alongside half the couples from our high school. Aggie was a town kid, so he'd settled on a trail ride through our sprawling acres.

I had to give him props for originality, and I really did want him to be happy, and the sales barn had a whole new crop of half-wild ponies to be whipped into shape, so I'd said sure.

When the ride went well, I pretty much left Quin to Aggie — heading off to ride other people's problem horses every day while my future sister-in-law exercised my own perfectly lovely boy.

The sweet boy who lowers his head for me to scratch his ears as though I've always been here to do it, and there's nothing I need to be pardoned for.

If anything will soften a heart, it's the forgiveness of a horse.

But I don't have time for the nostalgia that's been swamping me this last little while, so I snap the lead onto my horse's halter and say, "Come on. Let's walk."

Even though I didn't enjoy riding him, I did practice groundwork with Quin — using his good nature to help me pass my rider certification levels, and he still walks easily by my shoulder, matching my pace, with one ear turned to me and one flicking around to capture the sounds I can hear — birdsong, the chorus of crickets — along with many I know I can't.

We walk past all the buildings I've already explored, then I take him through the gap in the cedars down the worn path to the pond where I find a tidy scene — the fire pit cold, all trace of food and drink gone, and no straggling guests — most notably, my mother. I suppose Aggie and I probably owe a debt of gratitude to Brody and Gus for their efforts and, of those two, Gus is the bigger hero.

Fifteen minutes alone in a car with my mother who had consumed more than one martini and believed she'd been affronted. A shiver runs through me at the thought.

Quin tugs at the lead. "Yeah, yeah — you caught me daydreaming," I say.

I lead him around the pond, to a place where the grass grows particularly lushly and as he moves from spot-to-spot, head down, I lean against him and watch the sun come up and think I really haven't missed Vancouver at all, but even though I'm living in a trailer, I'd already miss this place quite a lot.

***

After a run, and a dip in the pond in lieu of a shower, and a bowl of Lucky Charms (from a box I bought for myself), I decide it's a reasonable time to make a phone call to BC.

Paisley answers the call yawning. "Is somebody dead?"

"What? Not that I know of."

"Injured?"

"No."

"Then why on earth would you be calling me this early?"

"You have to be up for work anyway."

"Hazel. It's Saturday."

"Oh. Shipwreck. I've kind of lost track of time."

"What did you just say?"

"Never mind. Sorry to wake you up."

"You're lucky I'm alone."

"Now that's not true. When was the last time a guy met the threshold to be allowed to sleep over?"

Paisley yawns again. "It's your mom's advice. It's ruined me."

The "just as easy to fall in love with a rich man ..."

"That's it. Ever since she said that I sit in restaurants and stare at the person I'm eating with and think, 'Is he rich enough to make up for the fact that he has only one ear pierced, or he calls pecans pah-kawns, or that he's a baseball fan?' and the answer is always, no."

"Yes, well, this is about my mom."

"Oh!" Her voice brightens. "I was going to roll over and go back to sleep, but stories about your mother are always worth hearing."

"Hmm ... well, get comfy and I'll tell you the latest ..."

"... so ..." I finish, after I've told her the story and explained my idea. "What do you think?"

"If you can get her here in the next 48 hours, I'll meet her at the airport. After that, I'm on my way ..."

"To the Gold Coast — I know — I want photos. And precisely because of that, I just want you to do a run-through of my condo. Hide my vibrator and lacy underwear at the back of my drawer. Put a carton of milk in the fridge if you have time. No chauffeuring expected. It was bad enough that Gus had to drive her home last night."

"Who's Gus?"

"Never mind. The point is, I'd never ask you to do that."

Paisley makes this noise she always makes when she shrugs her shoulders and says, "Your mother's always liked me."

"True. Better than she likes me."

"That's probably true. Sorry."

"No, it's helpful to have validation."

"Speaking of being helpful, and now that there's no way I'm going back to sleep — how goes everything?"

"Well, of course, my mom's just the same. My brother's pretty busy, so I don't see him much, but I think he's quite a sweetie."

"Hey, I always knew that."

"My sister-in-law might be better than I thought." I pause. "She's definitely different than I thought. I'm getting reacquainted with my old horse and, hang on, my sister-in-law just walked by. I should probably talk to her."

Paisley laughs. "I was more asking how you are."

"I ..." I think of all the things I could tell her that would be true, but not necessarily helpful. I'm confused. I'm conflicted. I'm sometimes sad for no reason I can pinpoint. I'm missing a feeling I never really had. "I'm not sure. I notice you haven't asked about Tom."

"I don't really care about Tom."

Her bluntness hits me with a sharp spear of relief. Maybe I'm not a complete monster to be able to walk away from my fiancé without looking back. I laugh. "I guess I don't, either."

"Well, that alone was worth the phone call. Now go talk to your sister-in-law and text me when you book your mom on a flight."

I jump down the stairs and head in the direction I saw Aggie walking. I find her at the side of the house, pegging laundry on a rotary clothesline. "Hey."

She glances at me before shifting her focus to untangling the sleeves of one of Brody's shirts. "How are you today?" I prompt.

She snaps the shirt out. "Well, your mom's not here, right? So that's better."

"Yeah. About that. I have an idea to run by you."

"Unless the idea is that we should sell this place and move somewhere far away where we can get a clean start, I'm not sure it's really going to work."

"It's kind of the reverse of that."

"Hazel, please don't mess with my head. It's the Saturday after the Friday barbecue. I might not have an alcohol hangover, but I definitely have an emotional one. And there's no rest for the wicked ..."

I turn to follow her gaze and see the kids arriving on a combination of bikes, scooters, and skateboards. "Mom, when's lunch?" "Mom, I'm starving." "Mom, Lynnie invited me over this afternoon, and her mom said they can pick me up in an hour, so we need to eat soon."

I meet Aggie's eyes. "It sounds like you need to make some food."

"You think?"

She's holding this improbably small pair of underwear. They're a light turquoise and they say **Monday**. Little-girl day of the week underwear. I had those. I look at Ali and wonder if she's wearing **Saturday** right now. There's a lump in my throat and my eyes sting.

I clear my throat. "Do you kids like grilled cheese?"

"Yes! Yes! Yes! Yes!" "But only with fake cheese!" "Mom won't make it with fake cheese!"

I lift my eyebrows. "Fake cheese?"

"The squares. Processed."

"Oh, well. I'll totally make it with fake cheese," I say, and while the kids are still cheering, add, "And, I put mayonnaise on the bread instead of butter."

"Ugh," Aggie says. "I'm going to pretend I didn't hear that."

"Correct. You just finish hanging up the laundry and I'll make some fake food for lunch, then we can talk."

***

"If you want to talk, you can come to the grocery store with me."

"It's not really what I had in mind. I was just there yesterday."

Aggie puts her hands on her hips. "You say that like you think it's what I had in mind. Like I woke up this morning and thought, 'Wow, I sure hope we're almost out of milk, and I spent a mere two-hundred-and-fifty dollars at the grocery store last time I went, so it only seems right to go and spend a bunch more.'"

I hold up my hand. "OK, fine, yes. I'll come to the grocery store with you, but I'm pretty sure that means I can't wash the lunch dishes."

"Aah ... the luxury of the single-tasking life. That's something else I left behind when I had children."

Who's the bitter one now? I have my mouth open to needle her with the question when Brody interrupts. "I got enough done this morning. I can stay in with the kids the rest of the afternoon and we can all do the dishes together. Why don't you two have coffee in the village after you get the groceries?" He digs in his pocket and hands me a ten-dollar bill.

I stare at it. I'm about to ask if he's also going to give me enough money to buy Aggie a coffee, then I remember — we're not in Vancouver anymore. I shrug and take it — "Thanks" — at the same time as Aggie says, "We don't need to spend money on coffee."

"Speak for yourself," I say.

She grabs a bundle of cloth bags, lifts a set of car keys from a row of hooks by the door, and on her way through the door calls back, "I would, if I thought anyone would listen to me."

***

"So, what's this great idea of yours?" she asks.

I don't answer right away. The country roads we're driving along are sometimes lined with sagging wire fences containing meandering herds of grazing cows. In between we enter tunnel-like stands of trees growing close to either side of the road. Then there are the occasional glimpses of the blue water of the great lake.

There are signs at the end of driveways, **Fresh Eggs for Sale**, and after we pass the **Welcome** board that marks the official entrance to the village, there are banners on the lampposts advertising the farmer's market every Saturday, and an upcoming summer festival, as well as reminding people not to litter.

It's so different from the city, and the West Coast. Both are pretty — many would even say Vancouver is more majestic — but I'm starting to believe the tugs of nostalgia are the universe's way of telling me this is home.

Aggie sighs. "Silence. Great. I could have had that by doing the groceries on my own."

Fine. She wants talk. We'll talk. "Let's talk about money."

"Excuse me? I thought you had some big idea to share."

"I do, but last night my mother made a comment about your finances ..."

"Your mother!" Aggie's hands tighten on the steering wheel and the car does a quick jerk-and-correct. OK, maybe I won't mention my mother again while she's driving.

"Yes, well, I'd normally ignore her, but you've also mentioned not wanting to pay for lunch out, or coffee, and how much groceries cost."

Aggie turns to stare at me, for just a little too long.

"The road?" I suggest.

"I'd like to focus on the road, but I'm too busy wondering what world you live in where people don't worry about the cost of eating out, or groceries."

I shrug. "If that's all it is."

Aggie's nose wrinkles. "Why are you interested? Are you worried about what's coming to you?"

Her question sets me back for a second. It may be true that some people don't think I'm the nicest person in the world, but my own financial situation honestly hadn't occurred to me. I guess it's true that I own half the farm, but I've always been happy to be a silent partner. To let Brody run it, figuring someone with a horticulture degree from the Ontario Agricultural College was more qualified than me. "Um ... if I was worried about what was coming to me, how worried should I be?"

"Not worried at all. You literally have nothing to worry about."

"Literally nothing ... does that mean ...?"

She cuts me off by putting on the indicator. "We're here!"

As we push the cart down the dairy aisle, I start. "So, I was thinking ..."

"Finally, I'm going to hear about this big brainwave of yours."

"Oh, well, not that quite yet. I was thinking about money."

"So, your idea isn't about money?"

"The original idea, wasn't — no."

"I'm suddenly much less interested in it." Aggie squints at the tiny print on the labels in front of two different kinds of cheese, and selects one. "About two months ago they re-sized all the cheese to four-hundred-gram bricks instead of five-hundred. But they didn't change the price." She shakes her head. "As if I wasn't going to notice."

"Since you did, and you're still thinking about it two months later, we really should talk about how I think you can make some more money at the farm."

Aggie pushes the cart away. "Let me guess. Offer bed-and-breakfast. Sorry to tell you, Hazel, that's not exactly an original thought in this county. Also, not sure if you noticed, but I fixed up the trailer and rented it out for Melissa Pritchard's wedding last year and the money was OK, but not enough to make up for all the extra work."

I catch up to her. "Exactly. As if you have time to make breakfast for total strangers. What you really need to do is film shoot rentals."

Aggie stops dead in front of the frozen vegetables and an older lady tuts and pushes her cart around Aggie's. "Film shoots?"

I nod. "Between the scenery and the outbuildings — the old sugar shack, particularly — there's lots of potential for film crews. And, even though the buildings would need some work done on them, it wouldn't be nearly as much as getting them in shape for bed-and-breakfast."

Aggie starts pushing again. She lifts a tub of yogurt off the shelf.

I decide to win her over by relating to her. Being on her frugal-grocery-shopping side. I point to a brightly coloured tub. "This one's a dollar less."

"That one's a-hundred-and-fifty grams smaller."

"It is?" I examine the one I'm holding and the one she's holding. "They look the same."

"Of course they do. It's an optical illusion. But I'm not falling for it."

"Wow. OK." I put my too-expensive yogurt back.

"So, the film shoot idea ..."

"Yes?"

"You'll probably think I'm really dumb, but I don't know anything about that."

"You're talking to somebody who can't tell the difference between two sizes of yogurt when they're both right in front of me."

"So, you're saying you don't think I'm dumb?"

"I'm saying I have a contact who arranges film shoots, so you don't have to worry about it."

***

Aggie hasn't brought up the film idea again, so when we sit down with our coffees at a tiny table on the patio of a coffeehouse in the village, I decide it's time to move onto Topic Number Two.

"What if I could get rid of my mother?"

Aggie chokes. She presses her napkin to her face. "You know listening to Canadian true crime podcasts is my guilty pleasure, right?"

"What? No! I'm not going to kill her. That would be a long-ass jail sentence."

"You know that now if anything happens to her, I'm going to have to testify about this conversation."

"How can you be a woman who one minute is worrying about a missing hundred grams of cheese and the next minute has steered a completely innocent conversation to murder?"

Aggie's examining her napkin now. "I'm pretty sure you made me snort coffee out my nose. Let me assure you the sensation is just about as unpleasant as it sounds."

"Oh my gosh, Aggie. Can we stop talking about murdering elderly women and huffing caffeine, and concentrate on sending my mother to Vancouver?"

I catch the woman at the next table staring openly, so I stick my tongue out at her.

Aggie gasps. "Hazel! What are you doing?"

"She's eavesdropping."

"That's so rude."

"Yes, it is."

"No. I mean ..." She sighs. "Fine. Whatever, I give up. What do you mean, send your mother to Vancouver?"

"Well, she's always saying how this place is too small-town for her, and I have an empty condo in Vancouver, and she's driving both of us crazy, so ..."

"Will she go?"

"Will she go to a big city, with lots of shopping, and tons of restaurants, and a theatre that hosts Broadway shows, and opera?"

"How, though?"

"Well, that's what we need to talk about, but it might blow Brody's coffee budget, because I think we're going to need another round."

***

The beauty of a tiny village is that everything's in walking distance. We left the truck parked at the grocery store and Aggie's gone a couple of blocks over to pick Violet up from her friend Lynnie's house while I'm nipping back into the store to buy two bags of milk we didn't want to leave in the heat of the parked truck.

I'm opening the back of the truck when I hear, "Oh, hello."

I turn to face Gus. "You're wearing a shirt," I say.

"So are you."

"I generally wear a shirt."

"Well, that makes two of us."

I catch him staring at the last-minute groceries I just got. I didn't bother with a plastic bag since I'm putting them straight into Aggies' bins. "Contrary to what my sister-in-law told you, almond milk is terrible for the environment, and I think soy milk tastes like ass. Believe it or not, I like my milk from cows."

"I wasn't looking at the milk."

"Oh." I'm also gripping a tub of Candy Explosion ice cream. The label suggests the ice cream itself is an eye-searing shade of antacid pink, and from what I can tell it contains gummies, bubble gum, chocolate bars, sprinkles — my teeth hurt just looking at it. "Yeah, that's to bribe my nephew."

"Bribe him to do what?"

"To like me."

"Is that the only way you can get people to like you?"

"Wow. You do think highly of me."

He glances at his feet. "I really don't like leeches." I follow his gaze. He's wearing flip-flops that show off narrow feet, with long toes. They look strong, and a bit rough — I can see callouses on his big toes — and his second toe's longer than his first one; isn't that a sign of intelligence?

Why am I more attracted to his feet today, than I was to his six-packed abs yesterday?

Then again, why was I able to leave my boyfriend-turned-fiancé of two years, literally without a second glance? How am I not worried at all about walking away from a job I wanted so badly that I started as an unpaid intern, working every night at a bar to be able to pay my rent, and ever since I've been on the payroll, have consistently worked sixty hours a week with this being the first "vacation" I've taken this year? Why is it so easy for me to plan to ship my mother out to live in the condominium I went without buying meat and alcohol for one year to save the down payment for?

I'm illogical, emotionally messed-up, and fickle.

I know that.

I also know his feet are really cute.

I shrug. "Well, it's a good thing I pointed it out, then."

"Oh, so you did me a service?"

"I believe it's called a 'kindness.' I did you a kindness."

"I guess I'm not familiar with the West Coast brand of kindness."

"Oh, there it is — I knew there'd be a Vancouver reference coming."

"Children, children, no bickering. I get enough of that at home."

We turn to face Aggie, returning to the truck with Violet skipping by her side. "Isn't Hazel resourceful finding you — has she asked you yet?"

Gus looks at me, and I look at Gus. "Asked him what?"

"About fixing up the sugar shack for your film shoot idea, of course."

"Of course ..." I'd pretty much assumed Aggie had already moved past my suggestion. That, if anything, she'd mention it later to Brody as an example of a very stupid idea I had. But looking at her face now, there's a brightness to it — a very different expression from earlier when her lips were pressed tightly together and she was rubbing her temples.

Maybe she respects my ideas, after all. Then again, I remember that the tight lips and rubbed temples came when the grocery cashier read out the total of the bill. So, it could be she just really needs the money.

Either way, it looks like we might not be able to move ahead. Or, at least, not with Gus's help.

"... pretty busy with building projects for the Gimme Shelter festival," he's saying in a matter-of-fact way, as though it's obvious what the Gimme Shelter festival is. Aggie and Violet are nodding, though, so I guess I'm the only clueless one.

I hate being clueless. "What the he ..." I catch Aggie frowning at me, "... *heck*, is the ... wait, is that the festival on the lamppost banners?"

Violet turns her head to me. "Yup! The school bus shelter festival."

School bus shelter ... "Is that why ...?" I'm flashing back to my realization, on the day I arrived, that *something* was different about the shelter at the farm. Since then the couple of times I've passed it, I've noticed that, indeed, it's half-painted and haven't given it much more thought other than it's a good thing my mother avoids going to the farm. When I was a kid, she wanted us to have a faux-Victorian school bus shelter, complete with gingerbread trim. My dad built the current, very plain, and very serviceable model which she disliked quite enough. If she could see its current patchy state, she'd have choice words. Words that would rhyme with "splashy" and "saidheck."

Violet nods more vigorously. "I painted our bus shelter for the parade. At least I started. I ran out of paint. But I'm going to finish it. I still have two weeks. Well, nearly. Ten days. Or over a week, anyway ..." Her nose and forehead are scrunching and she's biting her lip.

Another person with a problem.

I should just go. That's what I normally do when faced with other people and their problems.

But, for some weird reason, I want to help.

I rationalize that it's normal to want to support Violet. She's young, and adorable, and related to me by blood. She also likes me and the help she needs is timebound and simple.

Aggie, though. Adorable to my brother, I suppose, but not to me. She doesn't like me, and her problems are anything but simple.

Yet I'm leaning in, rather than turning away. *Bad idea, Hazel. You came here for a clean slate.*

I think of the advice I'd give a client – advice I'd charge them a lot of money for – "Walk away. Don't look back. Take care of you."

The thought doesn't give me the relief I expect. Instead I feel a race of panic.

Which, I suppose, makes sense. After all, the farm is half mine. And my mother ... well, as much as I hate the idea, I carry half her DNA.

So, it's in my self-interest to sort these issues out. Aggie's clearly not going to do it.

Coming from a place of superiority over my sister-in-law, and self-interest in my property portfolio, my urge to save the farm, and relocate my mother, make complete sense.

They're also considerably more pressing than a bunch of bus shelters.

I tilt my head and narrow my eyes at Gus. "Um, sorry, you're too busy doing decorating work for some silly festival to do paying work for ..." I'm thinking about the way Aggie reacted to his shirtlessness and am about to say, "your biggest fan," when I remember, for the moment anyway, Aggie and I are on the same team, and I probably shouldn't mock her. "... for actual pay," I finish instead, which is a very lame thing to say.

I hate being lame.

"*Silly!*" All three of them gasp and open their eyes wide as though I said something controversial like that kittens aren't cute (which they are), or that I don't like the Tragically Hip (which I do), or that it doesn't matter which way you put the toilet paper on the holder (which it does, so much so that I get a funny itchy feeling in my fingertips when it's on the wrong way that will only go away when I turn it around).

"The. Gimme. Shelter. Festival. Is. Not. Silly." Aggie says.

"It's not," Violet chimes in.

I turn to Gus. "So, it's like a real thing? Celebrating school bus shelters?"

"To the tune of raising ten-thousand dollars a year for the County's 'Bringing out the Best' fund."

Several snappy comebacks spring to mind.

"The best thing I've ever seen come out of a school bus was Carl Maddox's tuna sandwich that was stuck under the back seat for the entire school year," or, *"Does 'bringing out the best, include when all the people from Toronto bring their Teslas then complain that there's nowhere to charge them?"*

But I look at my sweet niece's face, and avoid looking at her mother's who I'm sure is itching to say, *"I'm sure you've never been accused of bringing out the best in anyone,"* and, instead, bite my tongue and reach for Aggie's arm. "First things first, let's get working on bringing my mother out of the province."

Seven

TORONTO IS NOT MY FAVOURITE CITY. Spending time with my mother is not my favourite thing. Yet I'm spending two hours in a car with nobody but my mother to talk to, and we're heading to Toronto.

She silenced my music early on. "I can't think with that racket in the background," she said as she picked up my phone and cut Gord Downie off just as he was singing about his feverish dream (see? I do love the Hip).

As I was wondering why she can't figure out how to do literally anything involving technology, but she can figure out how to shut off my Bluetooth in the middle of my favourite song, she started talking.

Since then it's been a monologue about the state of the government, the state of kids these days, the state of my troubled — and according to my mother, possibly alcoholic, possibly bi-polar, maybe suffering from early onset dementia — aunt, and the state of my aunt's marriage (not good, my mother suspects).

Phrases like, "I know you're not supposed to say it these days," and "I'm sorry, but I just have to give my opinion," pepper the diatribe.

"Oh, lord!" I yell.

"Well, I'm glad to hear you agree with me about that shyster in Centre Block ..."

It's really not worth it to tell her what I was actually reacting to was the highway sign telling me how close I am to the exit for the airport.

Whatever. I just turn on my indicator and move into the right-hand lane. I only have to listen to her for a few more minutes.

***

I have to admit as I make my way down Yonge Street, passing the clusters of businesses that make up distinct neighbourhoods — Mount Pleasant, Lawrence Park, York Mills — with the CN Tower winking in and out of view, I'm finding it easier than normal to like central Toronto.

It helps that on this Sunday morning I'm facing just about the lightest traffic you'll ever see in this city.

It also helps that before pulling out of the airport parkade, I sent a text to Paisley. **Incoming. Wheels down 12:12 your time. I owe you.**

I feel light and the traffic's moving and, when I reach the trendy neighbourhood where I have a meeting set up in an even trendier brunch spot, I can even find a parking spot. A free one. If that's not a miracle, I don't know what is.

Trent's waiting for me and, no surprise, he already has a heaping plate of food in front of him.

Trent is a bottomless-pit rugby player. He often says I saved him from starvation in first year university. Our meal plans were designed for an "average" student. Which meant by February he was out of funds, and I was facing the April expiration date having used only half my allocation.

My meal plan and I fed him for the remainder of the school year and he kept me from committing one of the biggest mistakes of my life by holding me back from the well-known-for-being-cruel, but also extremely charming professor I was teetering on the edge of sleeping with.

Sometimes it was verbal: "Come on, Hazel. Right now you have the power. If you sleep with that creep, you'll give it all away."

Sometimes it was physical: Trent could — and would — pick me up and carry me in the opposite direction from Prof. Shane's office.

Often it was through food: "Hazel. I'm starving. I need you to feed me. Right now."

Another first-year slept with Prof Shane. She got pregnant. He denied that he'd ever had sex with her. The paternity lawsuit and his very nasty, very public divorce were still in the news when we graduated.

When I look at Trent, I see someone who saved me, and also someone I saved.

He's tied with Paisley for the most equal relationship I've ever had.

Also, as I slide into my seat, he pushes a smoothie across the table to me.

He knows me.

"Wow, I've missed you."

"Then come to work for me."

I've heard him say it so many times it's become as routine and meaningless as "How are you?" or someone commenting on the rain in Vancouver.

Today I hear it though. The straightening of his spine and his lifted eyebrows tell me he notices.

"Is that why you've come? To finally put me out of my misery. Has the fiancé seen that the shores of Lake Ontario are much, much better than the Pacific?"

I sip my smoothie. It's slushy and fruity — just the way I like it. "Hmm ... there is no fiancé anymore."

"Oh." Trent lowers his knife and fork to the table. Considering there's still food on his plate, it's a bold move for him. "What happened?"

I trace a squiggle through the condensation on my glass. "I'm not completely sure."

"I'm sorry to hear that, but I will say it's important to be sure."

Trent does it again. They're simple words, but they lift a weight off me I haven't admitted I've been carrying. One of the reasons I haven't been thinking about Tom at all is that I didn't want to think about my unreasonableness, fickleness, unfairness — pick a word — in walking (driving) out on him. It was easier just to not think about him or our relationship, or anything.

There's truth in Trent's words though. I wasn't sure. If I wasn't sure, I couldn't marry him. It's pretty simple. There's no blame there.

"What?" he asks.

"I think you might have saved me again."

"Good." He's back to eating. Between mouthfuls he says, "I like it when you owe me. It's much the best position to be in."

"Well, after I tell you why I'm here, I think you might owe me."

"Oh yeah? Why's that?"

"I have a property for you. But not just any property. A *unique* property."

Trent, you see, is my film shoot contact. The one I told Aggie about.

Although the times I've worked with him it's been to find run-of-the-mill filming locations — ones that no viewer will notice. Ones that seem just like your average person's house except one notch nicer — like the way they say you should dress for a job interview, Trent's specialty is finding different, out-there, one-of-a-kind locations.

It's not that easy — he always says there's a reason "unique" and "unicorn" start with the same three letters. So, I'm pretty sure my unique/unicorn offer will grab his attention.

After he's done listening, he says, "OK. Sounds interesting. Potentially."

"Don't sound so enthusiastic. Don't you trust my judgment?"

He shakes his head, forks in a mouthful of hash browns and says, "Nah. Sorry Haze. If there's anyone's judgment I trust, it's yours. It's just there's other work stuff going on that isn't so great."

"Oh yeah? What happened?"

"My pet project blew up, that's what. Every year the firm dedicates twenty percent of our advertising budget to sponsorship, and the partners take turns finding a quirky, appealing, photo-slash-videogenic project to sponsor. This was my year."

I nod. I knew this. Last year they sponsored a woman who saved baby owls. On days when the city pressed in on me — when I didn't want to stand too near to the Sky

Train tracks for the paranoia that somebody would give me a good shove from behind, or I got tired of smelling everybody else's cannabis and food truck sausages, or when I made the mistake of wondering why I was working my butt off to rescue the brand of a business, or business person, who had destroyed their own image — I'd take five minutes and click on the owlet webcam and forget the world could be a shitty place.

Trent's explaining. "I thought I'd hit the jackpot. This peppy girl who had the perfect athletic-cute combo image. She was spending her gap year going across Canada swimming 15K a day in different public swimming pools to raise funding for building new public pools."

Before I can open my mouth to ask, he adds, "Fifteen kilometres times three-hundred-and-sixty-five days is five-thousand-five-hundred kilometres ..."

"... the distance across Canada," I finish.

He nods.

"Cute idea. I love it. Very social media, photo, and video friendly. And a different-but-worthwhile cause."

"All that," Trent agrees. "Until she started posting."

"Oh yeah?"

"Mmm ... So, apparently the reason she was taking a gap year is that she got accused of plagiarism in her final year of high school ..."

"Which isn't great, but ..."

"In five of her grade twelve courses."

"Yikes."

"And she was taking two spares and Phys Ed," he adds.

"So, in all of her academic grade twelve classes. Ouch."

"It gets worse."

"Do I want to know?"

"When the comments started showing up on her feed, instead of calling us for help, she told the commenters to go fuck themselves."

I cover my eyes.

"They said they heard she'd been doing her own fucking in exchange for getting her essays written for her, and she said, at least somebody would want to ..."

"She didn't!"

"Yeah, cute, perky, and quirky turned to foul-mouthed, nasty, and dishonest before she'd even symbolically swum her way past Butter Pot Provincial Park." He sighs. "Thankfully our sponsorship contract is rock-solid — we've hardly spent anything and we're off the hook but ... I just have to hope our brief tie to her doesn't go public, and we have a partner meeting Tuesday where I have to offer an alternative option." He shakes his head. "Anyway, that was a big tangent. Your property sounds promising and if you can send photos by

Tuesday, I'll share it in that meeting. At least it will be one small thing to redeem me."

"You'll have them on Tuesday."

When Trent's finished an additional side order of hash browns — "They serve the best ones here," — and I've downed my last mouthful of smoothie, and he's caught me up on his adventures trying to learn golf — "I still need to be convinced the business benefits are worth the blisters from my golf shoes and the mind-numbing conversation in the clubhouse," — I say I should be going and offer him a twenty.

He waves it away, but before I can stand up, he lays his hand on mine. "Haze?"

"Yeah?"

"If the things you're not sure about extend to your job, make sure you talk to me before you make any decisions."

"Really? You have an open position?"

"I'd make a position for you. Think about it and let me know if you're interested."

* * *

From carefree to care-filled in just under two hours and two-hundred kilometres.

However, while it's true I no longer have the balloon-like lightness in my chest I felt after dropping my mom off — while I have a lot of work to do if I'm going to send Trent pictures by his Tuesday meeting — this new weight

I'm carrying is worthwhile. It's one I took on willingly. It will be good for me if these things work out.

So, with no time to lose, and with the hood of my little car still warm from our return trip on the 401, I'm out in the late afternoon sun, using a scythe I found in one of my brother's sheds to hack a clearing around the sugar shack.

The next step is to clear most of the vines that have grown up along the posts of the porch. I'll remove the ones in the middle, that block the light and view from the windows and doors, and leave some around the edges since, to be honest, they distract the eye from the areas that need work. These include rotten boards on the porch, one of the stair treads pushed out of place by a sapling growing up behind it, and a cracked pane in one of the large windows that flank the main door.

It's hot, and the work is difficult. I'm sweating, and panting, and there's a persistent fly completing elliptical laps around my head, buzzing in and out of my hearing.

I take a vigorous swipe at a particularly thick patch of vegetation, swat at the fly, lose my balance and topple sideways. I scramble to get my hands underneath me — to push myself back up — when I'm distracted by the view from my landing spot.

Blue, blue sky. Lazy, white clouds. A bird so high it's just a silhouette like the kind kids draw — an upside-down W. The earth under my back gives warm, firm support to my hard-used muscles. I listen to my own breathing. My own heartbeat. I close my eyes.

I open them. "Oh my god!" I clap my hand over my chest as if to hold my thudding heart in. I blink, quickly, and the features of the person leaning over me come into focus. "Gus! You scared the sh … sugar out of me!" *Great, I can't even swear properly anymore.*

"I saw you fall. Then you didn't get up." He holds out a hand. "I wondered if you were OK."

I scramble to my feet without his help. Brush off my backside. "I was just fine until you nearly stopped my heart." With my eyes still readjusting after staring at the searing blueness of the sky, I squint. "What are you doing here, anyway? You said you couldn't come."

"I thought I might as well check out what needs to be done here."

"Hmm … I thought you had your super-important bus shelter work to do."

He narrows his eyes. "By which you mean you don't think it's super-important at all."

"Excuse me?"

"Well, there was no need for an adjective in that sentence. You could have just said, 'your bus shelter work,' but you chose to add 'super-important' for a reason. The only two reasons are as a straight-up, genuine modifier, or as sarcasm — like if I said, 'You strike me as a straight-up, genuine person,' which, of course, is sarcasm on my part."

Ouch. Was everyone around here always so blunt? Back in Vancouver people only insulted me behind my back. "Could there be a third reason? That I'm not as deeply obsessed with words as all that and I just plucked those words out of thin air without the deep meaning you're ascribing to them?"

He stares at me. Blinks. Takes a deep breath. "You're right. Somebody who uses the word 'ascribe' definitely makes their language choices lightly."

I roll my eyes. "Fine. I was casting aspersions on your school bus festival." I wrinkle my nose and stick out my tongue and repeat. "Aspersions. Yes, I said it. I suppose now you want me to say I'm sorry and I actually do think the festival's super-important."

He rubs his forehead. "To be honest, it doesn't matter what you, or I, or anybody thinks. There probably isn't going to be a festival, which is why I'm here, following up on this project instead, but I see you're already working on it."

I should ask him about the festival. I should show some interest. But I'm also kind of panicking that he's going to decide I don't need his help. Which, to be honest, I really do. So I bypass all the niceties and say, "Well, I'm working on the outside. There's a lot more work to be done, especially inside. I just got started because I need to take the first set of photos by end of day tomorrow."

"Ha!" He takes a step back and makes a sweeping side-to-side scan of the building which is, admittedly, more squalid than shipshape. "You don't want much, do you?"

"Oh, I want quite a lot. But in some areas I'll take what I can get."

By the time I'm finishing that sentence he's looking at me, and something about our eyes meeting while I say, "take what I can get" feels dirty, which I didn't mean it to, except, did I? Wouldn't I just drop his gaze if I didn't?

It's been a long time since I felt any kind of spark with anybody. So long, that I'm not sure if that's what this is, or if I'm just like some alpha dog using eye contact as proof that I'm in charge here. If so, my body's betraying me as a flush spreads through me. I automatically fan myself, then explain it away, "I'm hot." Is that really better? "It's hot." *You're hot*, I'm thinking and I don't want to say it out loud, so add, "The sun ... and I was working hard ... and I should be wearing a hat ... and ..."

"Hmm ... then maybe you should take a break from the sun and come inside with me so we can make a list of what needs to be done."

Come inside with me.

If only.

If only I could have a deeply lustful, fully physical, roll around on the unfinished floor with a wickedly fit carpenter, and have it mean nothing at all.

If only he wasn't a friend of my family, and if only I didn't need to maintain a somewhat professional relationship with him so he'll do these renovations for us.

If only ...

"Hazel?" He rubs his temples. He presses his lips together. He taps his foot on the ground. "I thought you were the one with the deadline."

Well I guess that puts me in my place. "If only" would only work if he wanted it too.

**

With my eyes closed I can appreciate the sound of the water lapping underneath the dock. The firmness of the wood supporting my spine. The softness of the breeze air-drying my still-damp hair.

Ever since I got back from Toronto both my brain and my body have betrayed me. As I lie here, cooling down by the pond, I'm supposed to be mentally adding up the costs for all the changes Gus and I talked over. I keep starting: *kitchen appliances – preferably second-hand, lumber and drywall to partition off the bedrooms, tiles to construct a wet room* ... and that's where my mind keeps veering off, replaying Gus saying, "I think a wet room would work here," and picturing Gus in the wet room with water running over his bare feet.

Don't go higher than the feet, I think. I know if I do, all bets will be off. It won't be just his feet I'll be picturing bare, and he won't be alone in my imagination — I'll be there, too — and I'm supposed to be figuring out what the renovation will cost. *Kitchen appliances ...*

It doesn't help that as I lie with late-evening fingers of sun falling across my body, lingering on my core, the warmth on my bikini bottoms drifts me into thoughts of Gus again.

"Oof!"

With my eyes closed there was no warning of the approach of Ali, landing astride my stomach, yelling, "I got my horsey, Patrick!"

"My horsey's better! Mine's standing up!" Sure enough, for the second time today I squint up to Gus outlined against the sky, this time with my nephew clinging to his back.

While his shirt remained politely on for the dinner Aggie insisted he stay for, everyone's since been in for a swim and Gus hasn't gotten around to replacing his top. My nephew's scraped and tanned hands are clasped firmly across Gus's chest which is several shades lighter than his arms and, if anything, just a little on the lean side of perfect ... which coincidentally is generally the way I prefer my men's chests ... *for goodness' sake, Hazel, do not let him think you're staring.*

"Scoot!" Aggie and Brody provide a welcome distraction as they advance toward us. My brother's clapping his hands. "Gus and Auntie Hazel don't want you climbing all over them. Come on!"

The kids leap straight into the pond, sending cold droplets splashing onto my warm skin. I sit up, Gus sinks down, and Aggie hands us each a plate of the strawberry shortcake she brought in a cooler, then lowers to the dock beside us. "So, is it true about the festival?"

Gus gives her a warm smile, which at first, I think is for the shortcake, then I realize is probably because she's taking an interest in the ridiculous festival.

You had your chance, says a little voice in my head. *You could have asked him back at the sugar shack.*

My chance for what? I counter. I'm ready to tell that voice, I don't need to impress this guy. I don't need his sweet smiles.

To one-up Aggie, the voice says.

Which, it has a point. I wouldn't mind doing that. I open my eyes wide, and tilt my head, and put my most inquisitive tone into my voice. "What happened with the festival?" See? I can take an interest.

"Of course the festival's *super-important* to me, but are you sure you care?" Gus asks.

"I asked, didn't I?" Whoops. That came out a little more snappish than I meant it to.

Aggie's not dumb. I'm sure she catches the tension between us, but of course she doesn't know the precise history. She answers. "The organizer had a heart attack."

"Yikes!" I say, "So much for a laid-back, fun festival."

"She didn't have a heart attack because of the festival," Gus says.

"You say that ..." I don't finish my sentence. Aggie's eyes are suspiciously shiny.

Gus notices, too. "Don't worry, Ags. Iris will be OK."

My sister-in-law tosses her hair back and swipes at her eyes. "Oh, gosh. Poor Iris. I know I should be thinking about her, but I can't stop wondering how we're going to manage without the Bringing out the Best funding from the festival. It covers half the costs of the school lunch program."

"Auntie Hazel could organize the festival." We all turn to face Violet who must have gotten tired of her solo swinging while we were all busy. "Mom said those ball caps you sent us were swag from a golf event you organized."

I swing my eyes to Aggie. I can just imagine her opinion of me sending freebies as gifts to the kids. "Wow, Aggie," I say. "It's almost flattering how much you seem to talk about me when I'm not around."

"Oh, you know …" she starts, and I cut her off, "I said it's *almost* flattering."

"Well, would it be flattering if I told you I'm sure you could organize the festival?"

"Hmm … well … first of all …" I hold up a finger, then notice a dab of whipped cream on it and pause to lick it off. I catch Gus watching me and stick my tongue out at him. "Wow. Yum. That is good …" Then I remember if I don't speak up soon I'm going to end up as the County's newest over-worked and under-appreciated volunteer. I take a deep breath. "As I was saying, first of all, I'm not actually working right now."

Aggie opens her mouth and I steamroller forward to keep her quiet. "And, even when I am working, event-planning is my least-favourite part of my job. Also — and I probably should have said this first — I know nothing about this festival which is in …" I look at Gus and lift one eyebrow.

"Thirteen days," he obliges.

"… unlucky thirteen days. Which brings me to the final, and impossible-to-argue with point, that nobody in this place has ever accused me of bringing out the best in anyone."

"But …" Violet starts.

Aggie interrupts. "No. Auntie Hazel's right. It's not fair to ask."

Which immediately makes me wonder if she's saying it's right that they shouldn't ask, or it's right that I never brought out the best in anyone.

Violet drops to her knees and leans against me. "You're wrong, you know."

Oh, her sun-warmed skin is so soft, and her hair, working loose from her braids, smells like pond water, and sun, and little-girl-sweat — like summer. I put my arm around her. "How am I wrong, honey-bun?"

"You brought out the best in Ali. She was nervous that strangers wouldn't understand that she's a girl, but you did, right away, and now she's not afraid for anybody to know."

The pang in my chest is excruciating. It's like somebody's scooped my heart right out and left an aching void behind, and if that had happened, my sweet niece would be holding my naked, beating heart in the palm of her hand.

"I'll do it."

Aggie gasps. Violet gasps. From the end of the dock Brody, with his arms resting on the wood, gasps. "You will?" everybody says — not quite in unison, but all in surprise.

Except Gus. He just nods.

I take a deep breath. "I will, except I'm not sure any of you have the authority to appoint me as the new organizer."

Gus nods again. "I think I can sort that out."

Eight

I'D FORGOTTEN THIS ABOUT ONTARIO. How at some point in the summer the nights just stop cooling down. How the air can hold more water than a sponge. How it wreaks havoc with my hair and my skin, so no matter how I try to control it, wispy curls spring out from my head, and my cheeks and nose shine all day.

How, once I'm awake wishing for a breeze that isn't coming, it's impossible to get back to sleep.

I yawn out of bed, yank a loose pair of shorts on under my sleep shirt, and step out of the trailer to find it isn't really cooler outside. Damper, perhaps, but that's not exactly appealing.

Coffee.

Surely even my early-to-rise farmer brother won't be up yet. I can tiptoe into the kitchen, brew myself some coffee and drink it on the farmhouse porch.

Or — my rule-following, high-achieving, long-conditioned inner voice suggests — since it's Monday and all, I could boot up my laptop and actually read my emails and make some sort of stab at figuring out how much of my life is left and how I can save it.

Who says I want to? I'd like to think the second voice comes from my spontaneous, rebellious, side.

In reality, though, it's prompted by exhaustion, burnout, and that deep and disquieting question — what's it all for, anyway?

I don't want to face my work responsibilities, I don't want to be mature about my relationship, and I definitely don't want to contemplate the meaning of life ... so I don't turn back to the trailer for my laptop.

I just continue along the driveway with gravel crunching under my feet and a looseness to my limbs that I haven't felt for a long time. It's the freedom that comes from being completely unobserved. From walking through the morning in the clothes I slept in. From having that wild humidity-curled hair and sticky skin, but it not mattering because there's nobody to see me.

Except there's someone on the front porch.

Shiza.

And sure as I've seen them, they've seen me. There's no turning around and going back.

Drat.

I suppose it might be nice if it was Brody. He's so busy keeping the farm running that I've barely seen him, and when he *is* around, so are dozens of other people — or at least Aggie and the kids.

It's not him, though. It's Aggie. Of course it is.

So much for morning solitude. So much for ignoring responsibilities.

Don't get me wrong — I know Aggie's probably thinking the exact same things. Which is why it's even more of a pain in the butt that we're stuck with each other now.

Because we definitely are.

"Hi," she says, with the same level of enthusiasm I'm feeling.

"Hi." At least she's holding a mug of coffee. Which means, sure enough, when I go into the kitchen there's already some made in the coffeemaker.

I realize I'm probably pouring what was meant to be Aggie's second cup of coffee into my mug, but, oh well — as my mother always says, "Nobody ever said life was fair."

I push back through the screen door and Aggie says, "Why are you smiling?"

"Am I?"

"Definitely."

"I was just thinking about my mother."

"About how she's in Vancouver?"

"That, exactly." I lower myself into the chair next to Aggie. "Paisley emailed me to say she's safely enthroned in the condo, and Paisley got her an appointment for later today at her manicure salon."

"So, she's happy?"

"Well, apparently she did feel my dish towels were past their prime ..."

Aggie's shaking her head. "I kind of understand."

"You understand about judging somebody based on their dish towels?"

"I understand how growing up with her could ... affect ... somebody."

"And by 'somebody' you mean me?" I blink at her through the steam of my coffee. Funny how there's no way you'd get me to take a hot bath in this heat, but I welcome the warmth radiating from my coffee. "Should I even ask what you mean by 'affect?'"

"It's too early to fight, Hazel. I'm just saying, you have a difficult mother."

"Brody does, too, and you love him."

"Brody's her son. It's different with mothers and sons. Besides, I love you."

Although Aggie isn't always my favourite person, I don't think she lies. She wouldn't say she loves me if she doesn't believe it. I'm tempted to point out she's always loved Brody, and that she doesn't love him because she has to, but because she chose him, but like she says, it's too early to fight.

I'll let her love me if she really wants to. "You love me enough to let me take your second cup of coffee?"

She sighs. "I guess I shouldn't have two before breakfast. Almost before the sun rises."

"Yeah. Hot one last night. Although the master bedroom was always the only cool place in a heat wave." When we were kids, my mom got my dad to install an AC unit in the window of their bedroom. Brody and I would sneak in sometimes to the cool room, darkened by the shutters closed to keep out the daytime sun. Depending how hot we were, it could be almost painful to feel the sweat suddenly sucked off our skin by the dry, treated air.

"Oh, there's no way I could do that." Aggie's shaking her head. "I was horrified when Brody told me about that. As if I could sleep in the cool and leave the kids sweating in their beds."

I open my eyes wide. "You know, I never really thought twice about it."

Aggie lifts her eyebrows. "Well, kind of like I said before, it's how you grew up." She shifts in her chair. "Anyway, that old unit's not up to much these days — we donated it to the community centre to keep the main hall at least tolerable in the hottest temperatures. Maybe one day we'll install central air, but as financial priorities go, it's pretty far down the list."

Ah, yes. The farm's finances. I need to spend some more time out at the sugar shack this afternoon before I take the first set of pictures to send to Trent. In the meantime, though ...

I stretch. "I don't really mind being up so early, but I wish I didn't have to get ready."

"What do you need to get ready for? It's just a low-key meeting in town with the festival volunteers ..." Her voice trails off, then she gets a sparkle in her eyes. "Or is it for Gus? There's a man who wears everything well, including pond water."

"I'm not even sure what that means." Except, even as I'm saying it, I'm getting a vision of pond water streaming off Gus's actually-quite-cut-if-unevenly-tanned abs. "What's his deal, anyway?"

"He was engaged to Tonya Watts. They met at university, and when she came back to help run the family winery he moved here with her. Then she dumped him for Bruce Jr. Gus has kept to himself ever since, but I got to know him through my volunteer work, and I really like him ..."

"And his soaking-wet aesthetic," I interrupt.

She shoots me a dirty look. "So we invite him over whenever we can."

"When you say Bruce Jr., are we talking about the son of my mother's boyfriend?"

"You got it. The tiny world of the County strikes again."

"And when you say Tonya Watts ... do you mean Tonya who drove the white Volkswagen Rabbit and ran the school fashion show?"

"Yup. That's her."

"But she was so mean." As soon as the words are out of my mouth, I hold my breath and wait for Aggie to make a comment about pots-calling-kettles or stone-throwing around glass houses.

I only realize I'm staring into the bottom of my coffee cup when Aggie's sigh draws my eyes back up. "More like cruel. Remember how the Valentine's candygrams were colour-coded — you were supposed to send pink chocolate hearts to girls and blue ones to boys? Tonya sent ten blue ones to Bridget D'Angelo."

"Oh ..." I feel like someone's kicked me in the gut. Bridget was one of the few people at school I was actually nice to. She was smart as anything and I was desperate to have her in my Model UN delegation. She was also very large, with a deep voice, and dark facial hair. I knew people were unkind to her, and I probably could have done more to stand up for her.

Aggie responds to my tone. "I know. I remember wondering what kind of person would spend ten dollars of her own money just to make somebody else feel terrible."

"I bet she didn't pay. If any of the guys in our grade were selling the candygrams, she probably gave them a blow job and they would have sent them for free." I wrinkle my nose. "Does saying that make me just as bad as her?"

"Nah. She used to brag about stuff like that." Aggie pauses, then continues. "Haze?"

"Yeah?"

"About Bridget. Well, not Bridget, exactly." She gives a long exhale. "Ali, actually." She looks right at me, and it's the first time Aggie and I have had real, proper, direct, eye contact since I got here. Come to think of it, it's the first time I've had real, proper, direct, eye contact with anyone for as long as I can remember.

Which, come to think of it, doesn't say a lot for my relationship with Tom.

"Violet was right," Aggie says. "You did bring out the best in Ali. Her journey has been — I guess, still is — a process for all of us, and we've dealt with a lot of reactions. Complete, absolute, don't-miss-a-beat acceptance is rare, and that's what you gave her."

"I don't know how else I would react. She is who she is. It's not up to me to have an opinion about that, or to try to change it."

"That's exactly what I'm talking about."

I clear my throat. "I'm not sure it's something I can take credit for, Aggie. It just seems like common sense to me."

"Well, you should know, it means everything to me."

I smile. "So, what I'm hearing you say is I'm not as mean as Tonya Watts."

She laughs. "I would *not* be happy if Tonya Watts was my sister-in-law."

I finish my last gulp of coffee. "All I can say about Gus, is if he's pining after Tonya, I'm not sure any amount of pond water streaming off his muscles could give me a favourable impression of him."

"Oh, so you did notice the pond water? And the muscles?"

As we're both laughing, a truck appears in the driveway. "Speak of the devil ..." Aggie says.

"By 'the devil' please don't tell me you mean ..."

She nods. "That's Gus's truck."

"Shoot!" I jump up. "I'm not wearing any undergarments whatsoever."

"I'm sure he won't mind."

"He's not going to have the chance to form an opinion. Give him a cup of coffee while I go back to the trailer through the trees. I'll be back in ten minutes."

"With underwear on?" Aggie yells after my retreating back.

I lift my middle finger and dive between the trunks of two spruce trees.

***

I admit it — I go into the Monday morning Gimme Shelter volunteer meeting feeling somewhat superior.

I mean, first of all, I've actually left this place and made a life somewhere else. And, for the past three years my company's made me the main organizer for the Artistic Endeavours Gala — a million-dollar-plus charity event supporting arts organizations in Vancouver. It's true I hate doing it, but *a million dollars*. I'd hardly have to get out of bed to handle a ten-thousand-dollar local festival.

Also, by some miracle, my five-minute dash to get ready this morning actually worked in my favour. On the grounds that I didn't have time to find anything that matched, or put on anything that needed ironing, I pulled on a black jersey tank dress which looks surprisingly good against the light tan I've acquired while spending time outdoors over the last few days.

The combination of the mounting humidity with the unwashed state of my hair has somehow conspired to create something resembling beach waves. They won't last past noon — soon it will all just be clumpy and oily — but for now I look urban chic and sophisticated and like I didn't try too hard (at least that last part's true).

At first glance the team is not at all remarkable — three women and, besides Gus, one man. Two of the women and the other man are what I would class as "normal" seniors — as in, not like my mother — they wear clothes chosen for comfort and hair cut for practicality. The third woman volunteer actually looks younger than me, but not in a go-getting way. I'm forming an image of her home. In my head it contains lots of inspirational pillows and even more cats.

All-in-all they look like they need a leader and I'm thinking how nice I am to have agreed to help them, and how much they can learn from me.

As Gus introduces me I smile, kindly, to take the intimidation out of his explanation that I've been living in Vancouver. That I work at a highly regarded boutique marketing and PR firm. My success with the arts gala (I used a broken pencil I found in his glove compartment to scribble these details on a Tim Horton's napkin I picked up from the footwell).

"... of course, now she's back home, living in her little brother's trailer, and I had to drive her here because I'm not really sure her tiny car is up to County roads."

I frown. That's a low blow. At least my car's not full of litter. Whatever. I'm not going to rise to his bait.

I turn my kind smile into a gracious one and bestow it on Gus, with a little pity mixed in for good measure. "The way Gus has described my living conditions it sounds like I might need to use this fund, so I guess I should make sure there's some money in it." I add a light laugh I learned from my mother. Very fake, yet always effective.

I haven't spent years in an agency that deals with big names, and people who think their names are bigger than they really are, without figuring out how to get them on side. Self-deprecating humour is step one.

Check.

Step two is to defer to them — or at least pretend to.

"Now, I'm just a newcomer here. You're the ones with the experience, so why don't you fill me in on everything I need to know?"

Check.

The two older women, who Gus introduced as Flora and Peace, exchange a glance. Flora gives a tiny nod and says, "Brenda, why don't you go first?"

Brenda pushes her glasses up on the bridge of her nose, clears her throat, lifts a hand to make a tiny adjustment to each of her earrings which — yes, I was right, are shaped like small cats — and I brace myself to smile through a hesitant, stumbling explanation of her duties.

"Well," she starts and I wonder if "well" is going to be her crutch word — inexperienced public speakers usually do have a word they use repeatedly. "Apologies to the rest of you who just saw this last week, but it's probably easiest if I run through the deck."

To nods all around, she opens a laptop, and a wall-mounted screen I hadn't noticed before lights up with a title page, **Gimme Shelter Parade**. "Actually, I do have an update," Brenda says. "Last week I said we had nineteen participants, but the new brewery, Beer on the Beach, is going to take part as well, so now we have a nice, even twenty."

The next slide is a detailed map of the parade route, and the one after that shows a spreadsheet with times plotted against specific locations along the way. Brenda isn't even referring to her slides. She's reciting information from memory and I follow along, reading that Brody's float, which consists of his tractor towing a flatbed trailer with four shelters on it, will pass Norm's Butcher Shop at 1:11 p.m.

There's no way I could take in all the information Brenda presents, but that doesn't matter because the main thing I take in is that she's on it. She has this entirely under control.

When she falls quiet and turns to me, I say, "Well. That was incredibly thorough." Clearly, I've also incredibly underestimated Brenda-the-cat-person.

Turns out she's not the only one. I mean, she's the only one with a PowerPoint, but the others are equally prepared.

Flora is in charge of the driving tour that winds through the country lanes so people can view the bus shelters in situ and vote for their favourites. She rattles off roads, addresses, directions, and even a construction detour. She briefly uses the screen to show the app she's adopted this year to allow the voting to be run and tabulated online.

I navigate to the app on my phone. It's slick. I've never heard of it. *OK ...*

Peace runs the market / merchant area that springs up on the Town Hall lawn which includes several "naked" bus shacks to be decorated onsite by the community, then auctioned off.

"One of the band members for the Tragically Hip bought one a few years ago," Flora tells me as part of her introduction of Peace. "The auction is our biggest earner."

As Peace explains the ins and outs of her responsibilities, it's quickly apparent that her "normal" senior citizen demeanour hides an artistic soul. The fervour in her voice when she discusses the meaning, symbolism, collaboration, and creativity the community puts into this activity make it sound like something worthy of inclusion in the National Art Gallery.

"I'm just the gopher," Kumar says. I'm clued up enough now not to believe him. I've realized nobody on this volunteer team is "just" anything.

"Oh no, Kumar." Flora shakes her head. "You're the nerve centre." She fixes her gaze on me. "Two years ago, when the prime minister decided to detour on his family holiday and bring his children to the Bash, Kumar was the point person dealing with his security detail."

I nod. "Message received," I tell her.

She smiles. "Good, dear. I'm glad."

"I only have one question left."

"Yes?"

"What do you need me for?"

**

Sitting in Gus's passenger seat, the binder Flora pushed across the table to me is heavy across my thighs. The edges of loose bits of paper are visible around the edges, but I'm not touching them. When I unsuspectingly opened the binder, there was a small explosion of receipts which were then caught by the currents of the ceiling fan, and it took everyone in the room to round them up. I finally got them all in such that they stopped falling out, and I'm not opening it again until I'm in a contained area.

"Iris isn't much of a numbers person," Flora told me. "Or a details person, either, come to think of it. The finances are a mess."

Given the incredible competence of the volunteer team, I was wondering what Iris really added to the running of the festival. But since Flora set me right about my assessment of the others, I decided it wasn't the time to question Iris's competency. Instead I said, "Like as much of a mess as this binder?"

She crossed her arms. "Let's just say, we could be making more money."

Message received again. It's my job to find that extra money.

Gus puts his indicator on. "I just need to pull over up here."

As he slows, I take a tight grip on my binder. If it slides off my lap there will be receipts lodged in places in Gus's truck that will mean they'll never be found again.

"Why?" My voice is sharp. I don't try to hide it. The only thing worse than the thought of tackling this bookkeeping nightmare, is the thought of not tackling it. Why do I have to be a part of Gus's little side trip? Why can't he drop me off where I can pour myself a cup of strong coffee, grab a calculator, and spread this paper out?

"This guy's had an old barn on his property taken down. He sold most of the barn board, but there are odd pieces left over and he said I can have whatever I want — no charge, I just have to haul it away."

"But, can't you ..."

"No."

"You don't even know what I was going to ask."

He arches the eyebrow I can see. "So, you weren't going to ask me to drop you off then come back?"

"I ... well, why can't you?"

"Because we're here."

Sure enough the truck is stopped in front of a stone foundation that must have once been a barn.

"And," Gus adds, "This is directly related to making the festival more financially successful, because these materials are free and they'll make the huts look really cool and people will pay more for them. And remind me, who's responsible for the finances? Oh, right ..."

"Yeah. Still not sure how that happened," I mutter. "Anyway, fine. You got your way, but I'm not helping. There's no way I'm disturbing this binder."

"Sure. Fine. Whatever." Gus opens his door. "It's just ..." He steps out. "Nah, forget it."

"What?"

"Oh, it's just that he said I could take anything at all, and I happen to know there was some pretty cool barn door hardware, and I think there's also a bunch of tin and I have some ideas for how I could upcycle them to use in the sugar shack reno, but ..." he points to the binder in my lap. "You can't get out, so it's no big deal. I'll just get the barn board for the huts and we'll get out of here."

I have a vivid image of the cavernous inside space of the sugar shack being divided into short-term-rental-friendly rooms, all partitioned with barn doors. I imagine the barn tin, cut in the shape of a kitchen backsplash, or into funky tiles for the bathroom. If those things are here, I need them. I sigh. "I feel like I spend my life saying no to you, only to then be forced to turn around and say yes."

"You know there's an easy solution to that, don't you?"

"Which is?"

"Stop saying no in the first place."

* * *

There's some amazing stuff here. Two entire barn door apparatuses, solid as anything, but with just the right amount of wear on them to show they're authentic.

And the tin. As soon as I saw it, I could picture the entire kitchen, even to the details of the lighting. We *need* that tin for the sugar shack.

Gus helps me slide the barn door hardware into the cab of the pickup, and the tin into the back of the truck. Then he tells me there's more barn board here than he needs for the huts, and with the extra he can build the actual barn doors to the size we need for the sugar shack.

"Are you only saying that so I'll help you load it?"

He stands back, hands on his hips, and slowly and deliberately looks me up and down.

I could protest, but it gives me a good excuse to do the same right back at him. Because of the humidity, his t-shirt — which reads *Gimme Shelter Festival* arched across an artistic rendition of a bus hut — clings to him in a couple of key spots. To me it's actually sexier than his streaming wet bare chest.

"Of all the things I might think of you, for some reason, I don't get the impression you're a shirker ... which is why I'm kind of surprised you're not working."

I lift my eyebrows. "Have you already forgotten the binder I had to climb out from under?"

"I meant, you know, paid work."

"What makes you ..." I pause because, actually, I think I know what makes him think I'm not working now. I noticed when he introduced me to the team he said, "worked" but I didn't think much of it. At the time I thought it was just a slip of the tongue, or a way of referring to something I did back in Vancouver which somehow doesn't apply while I'm on vacation here in Ontario.

If a vacation is what I'm on. I've never gone this long without contacting the office before. Even the couple of times I did take actual vacation, there was always at least some small crisis I had to wade in and solve. For all I know my job isn't still there waiting for me.

Given that I'm not even sure how much that would upset me, it's not worth correcting Gus.

Instead, I turn the tables on him. "I heard you were going to get married."

"I heard the same about you." Great. Right back at me.

Keep moving, Hazel. "You don't seem like the right demographic to be spending this much time volunteering for the festival — what made you get so involved?"

"Good question," he says. "What made you decide to get involved?"

OK, this tennis game has to stop at some point. Besides, I don't mind answering this one. "I didn't want to say no to Violet."

He nods. "She's a great kid. She's taken on a lot this year."

There's something almost proprietary in his tone that bugs me. It probably wouldn't bother a generous, well-adjusted person, but it does annoy me. Just because he occasionally has a burger at her house doesn't give this bachelor carpenter guy the right to talk about my niece. "You say that like you know her."

"Why wouldn't I?"

"Maybe because you're a grown man who shouldn't be friends with a twelve-year-old girl."

"I didn't say we were friends."

"What are you then?" I ask, but I've already decided. He's a creep. An over-familiar, presumptuous, creep.

"I'm her teacher."

"No you're not!"

"I'm pretty sure I am."

"You're a carpenter."

"Am I? Tell me how you know that."

"Because when I said we had to fix up the buildings at the farm, Aggie said, 'We can ask Gus,' and because I just loaded barn board into your truck for you to build school bus huts, and ..." I stop.

"And what?"

"And, that was pretty much it."

"That wasn't it at all. You were right in the middle of a sentence, then you stopped." He stops, too. Folds his arms. Waits.

I sigh. "Fine. You don't look like a teacher."

"Really? In what way don't I look like a teacher?"

I think of his bare chest, nicely defined even if skim-milk white. I think of the pond water coursing off his skin

... again. Every time I think of it the pasty skin becomes less important. I think of his feet, which I noticed at the time were really very nice, long-and-strong feet. Before my eyes can get too daydreamy, I say, "I can't picture you in chinos and a polo shirt."

"Oh, so you think I can't clean up well enough to be a teacher."

I shrug. "I didn't want to say it, but that's it, I'm afraid."

"That hurts. You'll see. Come September I'll get a sixteen-dollar haircut with a part, and I'll wear a lanyard around my neck with my ID, and I'll look the part, even if you don't believe I can."

September, I think. I'll be long gone by September. But, of course, facts don't matter when you're just shooting the shit like we are.

"Come on," he says. "I'll get you home so you can talk to Violet — *my student* — and she'll set you straight."

Nine

ONTARIO.

You're basically not allowed to say you love it when you live in BC. It's not done. It's like saying you don't like to travel, and exercise isn't hard work — you like it, and that you don't need a glass of wine at the end of a hard day. People raise their eyebrows and mutter to each other, "She's just saying that for effect."

Also, to be fair, I didn't realize how much I loved Ontario until I'd been in BC for so long I'd almost forgotten it.

But I do. Now I know why I was having all those nostalgic flashbacks. My body was trying to remind my brain — *We lived in a good place before. It's still there. We can go back.*

I love the woods and the meadows. I love the water (fresh — not salt!). I love the abundance of wildlife, with most of it much less likely to kill you than anything in British Columbia. I mean, sure, we have moose here, and you definitely shouldn't mess with a moose, but they're not predators. If you have any smarts, you can absolutely avoid moose run-ins.

I especially love all of it from the back of a horse.

This is what Quin was built for. Gentle trail rides through a misty morning. Carrying me through the blossoming of the day with my hips following his four-beat walk rhythm. Sighting the duck-covered pond between his pricked-forward ears. Sending those angrily quacking ducks on their way by wading right in and splashing away their morning tranquility.

As we head back, with the late-summer air wicking the pond moisture off us, I drop the reins and steer Quin with my legs and my seat, and he responds with his usual good manners and receptiveness.

I think about the bus shelter festival parade. I lift a hunk of Quin's long mane. I eyeball it and imagine it braided through with sparkly ribbon. I wonder if the kids could help me stencil **Edwards Farm** on a saddle pad.

Free advertising. That's why I'd be doing it. Not because the closest I've ever come to riding a horse in a parade is putting my childhood Barbie in a fake parade on her plastic horse and wishing it could be me.

Hmm ... maybe all the kids could ride with me. Well, not Violet, obviously. At least, not on her devil-horse ...

The scream jolts me back out of the world of sparkly braided horse manes and Barbie parades.

Quin's ears shoot forward and he gives a snort. I close my legs around him and he hesitates — horses haven't survived through all these millennia as a species with no claws and blunt teeth by rushing into situations involving screaming.

Still, he's a well-trained boy so when I cluck and say, "Come on, we have to go find out what's happening," he gives a different kind of snort — one of resignation — and accelerates into a jouncy trot, then a quick canter.

Patrick's sitting on the porch steps with a white cloth quickly turning red wrapped around his hand and his flushed cheeks rapidly draining to white.

"*Shi*..." I start, before instantly converting it to, "Shiver me timbers!"

Aggie glances up and the fact that she doesn't even start to warn me about my language tells me all I need to know about her state of mind. "Thank goodness you're here!"

I jump off Quin. "What happened?"

Ali pipes up. "Patrick was practicing to get his knife permit for when Cubs starts again, except he practiced too hard and sliced right into his ..."

The whiteness of Aggie's face makes me say, "OK, Ali, that's enough detail. I get the picture."

"It's deep," Aggie says. "He needs to go to the doctor. Brody's already in the fields and I can't call him back. It's going to rain tomorrow — he has to get the hay in ..."

She's interrupted by Violet stepping out onto the porch holding the kitchen phone. "It's Julia's mom. She says Ali can go to the beach with them for the day." Violet hesitates. "She says I can go, too ... but ..." she wrinkles her nose.

Aggie rubs her forehead. "Honey, I know you don't want to hang out with a couple of nine-year-olds all day, but do you really want to come to the ER with us? It could be a very long wait."

"Or," I say. "She can come to the city with me."

Everybody stares at me. "I'm meeting my friend, Trent, for lunch. You know — the one with the film crew connections — he's nice. You can join our meeting and eat with us."

"Really?" Violet asks.

"Really?" Aggie says.

"Yes, really, but your mom needs to go with Patrick ASAP, and we'd need to leave not long after that, so you'd have to help put Quin away, and get Ali ready for the beach ..."

"I can do that!" Violet's running down the stairs before I even finish talking. She grabs Quin's reins. "I'll untack him and turn him out right now!"

I turn to Aggie. "Go."

She looks at Patrick whose bottom lip is quivering. "I'm afraid to look at it, Mommy."

"Go," I repeat.

She nods. "OK."

Then, while she gets him into the car, I run inside, grab the box of Lucky Charms and put it in the backseat next to my nephew. "In case you need a snack," I say.

He looks at me. Whispers. "Thanks Auntie Hazel."

"No problem, bud. Eat as many as you want. I'll buy you another box."

***

We've stopped for gas once and pees twice — mostly because on the first pee stop we also bought drinks. Now we're on the final leg of the 401 into Toronto and Violet is swiping through the first batch of sugar shack photos I took.

"So, we're going to show your friend the photos of the sugar shack?" Violet asks.

"Among other things."

"But ..." She shoots me a sidelong glance.

"Yes?"

"Well, if they're on your phone, why do we have to go to the city to show him. Why didn't you just send them?"

"I actually did send them, because he's using them in a meeting he's probably in right now, but yesterday Gus and I talked about a couple more things, and I want to meet Trent in person to talk about those."

"Gus," Violet says, and smiles. "It's OK for me to call him that in the summer, but in the school year I call him Mr. Perry."

"Right," I say. "Because he's your teacher."

Violet nods. "We have split classes so we get the same teacher for two years. I'm so glad I'll still be in his class in the fall. He was the person who helped me the most about Ali."

"How did he help?"

"He told me his room was a safe space and I could come there any time. I could even bring Ali if she wanted to come — even though she's only in grade four. He said I could tell him anything and he'd listen."

"And did you?"

She nods. "I'd mostly read my book and eat my lunch while he marked. And whenever I didn't come he said, 'Hey, that's good with me — I think it means you're having a good day.'"

"That's nice." As I say it, I'm thinking of not-nice me giving him a hard time about being a teacher. It's so clear to me now. Nice Gus Perry being a nice teacher to kids who need him. I bet he can even rock a polo shirt and a pair of chinos. Of course he's a teacher. How could I ever have doubted it?

"So, you like Mr. Perry? I mean, Gus?"

"Violet, if he makes you happy, I love him."

I don't think she's listening anymore, though. She points across the seventeen-or-so lanes of midday Toronto traffic. "Is that a wind turbine?" Her eyes widen. "Oh! Wait! Is that the CN Tower?"

Her head swivels for the rest of the drive downtown and as we walk from our parking spot to Trent's office she never stops looking up, down, and side-to-side. She stays very close to my side. Her nose wrinkles, "It smells funny."

"Mmm, yes." The big-city smell of weed and sewers. It's slipped to the back of my mind. I haven't missed it.

Violet's eyes go the widest yet when Trent shows us into a meeting room with one entire wall of glass. "Is that the CN Tower?" she asks for the second time today. Then she turns to the huge table. "Is that Subway?"

There are two platters — one covered with half subs, one holding lines of cookies — with a row of canned soft drinks beside them.

"Yes. Sorry." Trent shrugs. "Our intern is clueless. When we sent her out for sandwiches, she brought back Subway."

"I love Subway!" Violet says.

"Have at it, then," Trent offers.

"So," he turns to me. "As much as I love to see you — twice in a week — you did send me the photos so I'm not quite sure why you're here."

Violet, mouth stuffed full of turkey breast sub, waggles her eyebrows at me.

"Violet," I say. "I need to go to the bathroom. Why don't you tell my friend Trent about the Gimme Shelter festival?"

While my good-natured, rule-following niece nods and swallows the last bite of her sub, Trent mouths, *What are you doing?*

"Just listen," I say and push through the door.

I take a good, long time in the bathroom — humming Happy Birthday twice while I wash my hands. I wander by the reception desk and congratulate the intern on the variety of subs she picked up. In the hall back outside the meeting room I peek through the glass panel in the door. Violet's still talking. I was pretty sure she would be.

Trent pushes the plate of cookies toward her while he asks her a question. I can see her eyes flicking back and forth between the chocolate chip and the white chocolate macadamia. It's plain that talking to Trent while trying to choose which cookie to have is far too much to expect.

I take pity on her and push into the room in time to hear her say, "...the year the prime minister came, and I got to have my face painted with his daughter ..."

Trent turns and looks me straight in the eye. "Yes."

I nod. "Right?"

"Absolutely right."

"What?" Holding her half-eaten cookie Violet looks from one of us to the other.

"We've just solved two of our problems in one go."

"Oh?" She looks confused until I say, "Why don't you solve your problem by having one of each kind of cookie?"

***

On the way back to the car we stop at a souvenir shop. Violet picks a knock-off Raptors t-shirt for Patrick. "Should I get him something extra? Because he got hurt?"

"Your mom texted me while we were at Trent's. They're back home and your brother's going to be OK — he just can't get his hand wet, so no swimming for a bit. It's been a big day, so I'm going to buy us pizza for dinner. That will be an extra treat for everyone."

"Do you think Ali would like this?" Violet holds up a vividly beaded rainbow pin in the shape of the CN Tower.

"I know I love it."

With her own, identical pin stuck on her t-shirt, Violet sits in the passenger seat and keeps a running commentary on the people driving around us.

"That lady has a cat in her lap."

"Very dangerous," I say.

"That man has his hand sticking out of his window."

"Also dangerous."

"I've never seen a car painted that colour before."

I check out the matte-purple car in question, also sporting a homemade spoiler. I suspect the purple paint came out of a can in somebody's basement. There are clear paintbrush marks on the body.

"You probably never will again."

"What two problems did you and Trent solve today?"

"Ah. Well, we actually solved three, or four, depending how you look at it."

"What are they?"

"Well the film shoot one. You saw us looking over the photos of the outside of the sugar shack together? He liked them enough to recommend it to his client. So that's good for the farm — because the client will pay — and it's also good for Trent, because it can be hard to find good locations for filming." I don't mention that I also promised Trent some interior shots for his client presentation by noon tomorrow. I'm happy to just stick with the "problem-solved" narrative for now.

"OK, so that's two problems solved," Violet says. "What about the rest?"

"Trent's company is going to sponsor Gimme Shelter."

"They are?"

"Yup. Thanks to you and the great way you described it to him."

"But, wait, how do you know? I didn't hear him say that."

"I knew he was looking for an event like the festival to sponsor, and now that I'm in charge of the festival's finances, I knew it needed money ... and how much it needed ... and I already knew how much Trent's company had for the sponsorship, so I knew if he heard about it from you, he'd love the idea."

"So, you just know?"

"More or less. Trent and I have been friends for a long time. He'll email me a bunch of forms and I'll fill them out later today, but — yeah — about this, I knew."

"I have one more question."

"What?"

"How do you know which way to drive in this great big city?"

***

I have another Ontario moment as I turn the car back onto the rutted farm road. As my day started, I felt like nothing could be more beautiful than the morning light, but now the late afternoon has proven me wrong.

With the oppressive humidity broken, the air's soft and welcoming. As soon as we got off the highway, I rolled the windows down and it seems my brother's not the only one haying today — the breeze is permeated with the fresh-cut smell.

The crickets sing — or that could be frogs — or both, with some birdsong backing them up.

Violet is dozing in the passenger seat, but as soon as the car rolls into sight of the farm driveway — and, specifically, the bus shelter at the corner — yells go up, "Auntie Hazel!" "Violet!" Ali and Patrick bounce to the edge of the road. They're both holding broad paintbrushes, dripping paint, and both grinning. Patrick's hand is bandaged, but I assume he must be fine to be jumping up and down the way he is.

"You guys!" Violet's eyes open wide as she takes in the broad pink and blue stripes on the hut. "You're finishing it! Can I help?"

Ali nods as we come to a complete stop so Violet can step out. "We started with the bottom because that part's easiest for us to reach. You can start on the next stripe up …"

I'm thinking it's surprising Aggie let the kids loose with paint, when I catch sight of a denim-clad backside bent over a drop sheet dotted with paint cans.

A backside that's familiar but not-at-all-boring.

Gus straightens, holding a loaded brush out for Violet. "Here you go ma'am. Have at 'er."

I blink, first because of the wave of emotion that hits me then, again, more quickly, because I don't want Gus to notice. How could I explain to him that I've been suddenly done in by my nostalgia again — by the late-day summer feeling you can only get in the countryside, by the sight of kids very much like me and my brother laughing over a messy project (although in our day, the project would never have been painting a bus shelter in the colours of the trans flag), and to top it all off, by that quintessentially small-town phrase, "have at 'er" — you don't hear that in downtown Vancouver.

As Gus's gaze falls on me I lift my hand, point down the drive to my parking spot in front of the trailer, and coast the car into place.

Engine off. There. Done. A long day over.

The kids' voices rise and fall behind me and I try, try, try to grope myself back to that fleeting flash of nostalgia. It's such a hard feeling to live with — so sweet it hurts, and so painful I feel the need to blink it away. These nostalgic episodes I experience are rooted in the deepest sadness while being some of the happiest moments I can remember.

And now I've rushed past it and I can't get back and I'm left sitting here in my car thinking about all the things I have to get done.

Sure, I sold Trent on the sugar shack ... but now I have to get it ready. And I did have a moment of self-congratulating when he agreed to the sponsorship ... but that means I need to actually run the festival. And those are just my responsibilities in this temporary, Ontario-based life I'm living. At some point I need to face my job, and my fiancé, if only to figure out how I'm going to feed myself and what I'm going to do with the rest of my life.

That's all.

I think I'll just go into the trailer and lie down and see if I can sleep right through 'till tomorrow morning.

Or, maybe I should just give up and go back.

I picture Tom lunging at JJ.

OK, not to Tom, of course.

I imagine spending a day making up nice things to write and post about Lily Rothman, to push her intoxicated escapades off the first page of Google results. Then I think of writing her med school application. My stomach churns.

So, obviously I couldn't go back to my previous job.

I envisage parking my car in its underground spot. Riding a chrome-and-mirrored elevator to my concrete-and-glass condo. I think of the mountains pressing in and the salt water surrounding the city.

It's for some people – but it's not for me.

So, back to the sleep-until-I-wake-up plan.

"Hazel?"

I sit very still. Aggie might not have seen me. Maybe she just noticed the car's back and is calling out in this general direction to see if I'll answer. I hold my breath. I stare at a bug mark on the windshield — one of many that will only wash off the next time we have a long day of continuous rain. *Be invisible*, I think. *Be one with the car.*

"Hazel?" Yeah, so that didn't work at all. Her voice is right next to me now. "Are you OK?"

I sigh, slide my eyes sideways and up, to meet hers. "Fine. Just ..." Words fail me, but Aggie laughs.

"Just trying to ignore the world and hope nobody will bother you for a while?"

It's one of those moments when I actually completely like my sister-in-law. "I'm not going to deny it."

"Well, I'd absolutely back you up on that, but Gus spent most of the day working at the sugar shack and he wants to talk to you, so ..."

"Yeah." I undo my seatbelt. "OK." I crack the door open. "Guess if he worked all day for free the least I can do is talk to him."

"I have an idea," she says. "How about we all have dinner first, then you can go check out whatever he wants you to. I wouldn't want you to get hangry."

"You know, I'm really not sure my bad temper can be blamed on being hangry, but it's nice of you to give me the excuse."

***

Maybe I was on my way to being hangry. Or, at least, experiencing a low-blood-sugar energy deficiency.

Because after the kids have marched up to the house, and bickered all through washing the paint off their hands, and once I've had my fair share of the massive lasagna Aggie made to give Brody a solid meal after his long day in the hay field, I find I have the energy to volunteer to wash the dishes. Gus plays several hands of crazy eights with the kids while Aggie and Brody sit off to the side and drink a cup of tea together.

The old farmhouse sink is so deep I'm nearly up to my elbows in dishwater and it takes me right back to Thanksgivings and Boxing Days. To the informal get-togethers driven by my dad. He'd invite old friends and close neighbours and after a few glasses of wine my mom would relax enough to forget that she didn't like potluck suppers. I'd take my turn at the sink — this sink — part of the rota washing a seemingly endless parade of Pyrex dishes and pie plates. The room would be full of other people — mostly women — carrying in dishes, scraping them over the compost bin, washing, drying, stacking. Laughter-sprinkled conversations rose and fell all over the main floor, and occasionally something would run into my leg and I'd glance down to see somebody's dog, or their toddler, doing circuits through the party.

Then I moved out. By myself. I thought I wanted a cleaner, simpler life. I got that life.

And now I'm back here and surrounded by dishes and the people that ate off them, and it feels good.

The ringing of the phone breaks the atmosphere.

It's the same phone that hung on the wall when I was a teenager, and there was a time when I would have run for it. When I thought it might be the sales barn saying they got in a trailer load of newbies and needed me to come right over and give them their first rides, or someone from the recruiting offices of any of the universities I applied to offering me a scholarship, or really anyone at all with any kind of offer that would take me somewhere bigger, more important, and less claustrophobic than this farm tainted with the constant low-grade unhappiness of my mother.

It's not my house, though, and as aforementioned, I'm elbow-deep in sudsy water, so Aggie gets it and I'm happy for her to do so. Until she says, "Um, ye-e-es, she's here."

I'm already shaking my head because no good can come of this. Pretty much everybody in the world I'm on speaking terms with is in this room right now. Except Paisley, and by my calculations she will have landed in Australia for her conference where it's about midnight tomorrow.

Aggie lifts her shoulders in a "what am I supposed to do?" kind of way and I sigh, and shake my hands dry and accept the receiver. "Yes?"

Oh god. I was right. It's Devon. "You didn't have an appendectomy."

Deflect. It's what we teach our clients to do if someone confronts them with something they don't want to deal with. "Is that a question?"

"It's a fact."

Delay. We also teach them that. Except, in this case it's less a delay and more a long period of silence as I notice everyone in the room has stopped what they're doing to stare at me. As if I can think with six pairs of eyes on me. Thank goodness for the stretched-out phone cord. I step around the corner into the hallway where I face the wall.

Devon's already talking again. "I should fire you. I would fire you if you hadn't earned me eleven times what I paid you last year."

"That's very specific."

"I did the numbers, Hazel. You know I don't make decisions on emotion. Right now the money's in your favour, but even that won't save you forever."

Fine. Do me a favour. Cut me loose. The thoughts surprise me. Is that really how I feel? You might think it's because of Devon's hostility, but that's Devon. Hostile is his base state. It's never bothered me. In fact, it means I've never faced any pressure to indulge in the kind of rah-rah team-building activities that make me shudder when I read about other offices doing them on LinkedIn.

Our all-business-no-personal workplace has always suited me. Our generally unlikable clientele has made it easy to fix their (usually self-made) problems, take their money, and forget about them … until they mess up again, which most of them do.

The pay is good.

I've never thought of leaving.

Until now.

"You have until Monday."

"I have until Monday for what?"

"To be back here, at your desk, making money for the company."

OK, wait a minute. Maybe I don't want to leave. Or, at least, maybe I don't want to be unemployed. "It's a five-day drive."

"It's a five-hour flight."

"I have my car."

"Well, I've given you six days, so if you insist on driving, that leaves you a whole day to pack and say goodbye."

When I don't respond immediately, Devon continues. "It's non-negotiable … just in case you thought I was negotiating."

"I've never thought you'd negotiate, Devon. I do want to know one thing, though."

"Which is?"

I look at the cord wrapped around me, attached to a landline that isn't even in my name. "How did you find me?"

He snorts. "Don't insult me Hazel."

It's how our conversations often end, and from the dead air it's clear this one is over, too. Devon's not one for wasting time once he's said what he wants to. I push the hook down with my finger so I can leave the receiver pressed to my ear as Aggie stampedes the kids past me. I smile. I nod. "Yes, yes," I say. "Of course." I make a mental note to come up with a story about what I was agreeing to in case one of them asks later.

While I'm smiling and faking, I think Devon's right — it's actually a miracle that it took this long for him to track me down. Of course he probably only started looking recently. I wonder why he started looking. I wonder who else knows I'm here.

I don't want to think about it.

I want to see the sugar shack. Even though I'm skeptical about how different it can be considering the short amount of time Gus has had to work on it, and the zero budget he was working with, this thing has returned with my nostalgia — senseless optimism. The same thing that kept me hoping that I'd find exactly what I wanted under the tree every Christmas — instead of what my mother wanted to give me. Or that I'd meet someone who'd look at me the way my brother always looked at Aggie — even way back in high school.

I never let anyone know I hoped for those things, and they never happened, but a part of me kept thinking they could ... maybe ... it wasn't impossible.

Now, that part of me wants to see the sugar shack. I unwind myself from the cord, hang the receiver on the hook and burst into the kitchen saying, "OK, Gus! I'm good to go. Show me this sugar shack."

I stop in the doorway. The room's empty. Of course it is. My mother will never see me for myself. Nobody will ever adore me the way Brody adores Aggie. My boss tracked me down more than halfway across the country and he might fire me, and if he knows where I am, my ex-fiancé might too.

And the guy I've been not-very-nice to about his efforts on my behalf fled the vicinity while I was in the act of being near-fired.

Why wouldn't he?

This is one of those moments where I could be sad, or I could be mad.

Being mad hurts less, so I jam my feet into my sandals, slam the screen door, and stomp along the gravel path toward the sugar shack, muttering *Goddamn teachers who think they're carpenters ... under my breath.*

***

I grumble to myself for the first part of my walk:

"Stupid Trent ..." I gave him charming — if somewhat soft-focused — exterior pictures. Why aren't those enough?

On the narrow path through the trees, the light's already dim. I stub my toe on a raised tree root.

"Stupid Gus ..." He got my hopes up when I know, realistically, the time it takes to drive to Toronto and back isn't long enough to transform the shack, and now I'm going to have to be nice to him about whatever little progress he's made.

Something scuttles across the packed dirt trail and sends my nerves skittering on edge.

"Stupid me ..." Why did I get involved in all this? Why did I come here? Why am I trying to make money for the farm? Why did I reach out to Trent? Why did I say I'd help with Gus and Aggie's festival?

A dark shape flits out of the tree canopy and I instinctively duck.

My work-obsessed, results-focused, unencumbered life back in the city was simple. It was easy. I might have worked a lot, but when I didn't work, I only had myself to worry about. Why did I mess with that?

Because I was lonely.

Just thinking the words is enough to stop me in my tracks. To send my hand flying to my breastbone to press against the sharp pain pushing up from underneath it.

No. I wasn't. Was I?

I lift my eyes to the darkening sky with the first stars already pin-pricking it and am reeled right back to childhood camping trips. My dad finishing a long day of work in the fields, then packing Brody and me into the pickup.

We'd be allowed a rare stop at McDonald's and would arrive at our campsite with daylight fading quickly. It was all hands on deck to get the tent up, get the sleeping bags unfurled, and light the first campfire of the trip. After that mad scramble we'd sit in camp chairs pulled close to the fire pit, roasting marshmallows, listening to the crackling of the burning logs, and feeling the cold air on our faces when we turned them away from the flames and up to gaze into the star spray above.

Stop, I think. Stop thinking of my dad, who's gone. And my brother, who has his own life now. And this place which, if the finances are as dire as Aggie keeps hinting they are, might belong to somebody else before long.

"Hazel?" My name, called out loud, silences the voices of the bugs, and birds, and beasts of the night. "Hazel? Are you out there?"

Gus's voice reminds me why I'm here. To despair at the state of the sugar shack. To be annoyed with him. To be distracted by the outward demands and difficulties of everyday life so I don't have to tune my thoughts inward.

It's what I'm good at. It's what I've been doing all these years.

"Oh yes!" I call. "I'm coming!" And it's definitely more of a threat than a promise.

Ten

WHAT THE ...?

I stand on the main trail and gaze along the path leading to the shack, and I *can* gaze along it because it's lit the whole way.

Low-profile lights with a crackle finish pool warm illumination onto — "Are those flagstones?" I'm asking myself, but the answer comes from a shadowy figure standing on the porch.

"Brody and I dug them out of the shore when we built the deck at the pond. I thought they might come in handy sometime."

The irregular-shaped, flat flags form an enchanting walkway to the porch, still natural enough to look organic between the long grasses and wildflowers on either side, but defined enough to invite — almost beg — me to step along them to the sugar shack.

When I get to the low set of stairs, the diffuse glow of the lights and the wash of the nearly full moon pick out a couple of boards much brighter than the ones around them. I put my foot on the lowest one and, sure enough, it holds my weight, doesn't creak, doesn't give.

"Wow," I say. "No chance of falling through."

"Well not right in front of the door, but I wouldn't venture too far to either side." The same light that illuminated the new boards emphasizes the white of Gus's teeth.

The door.

It's exactly the way it should always have been, which is painted rustic red. I can see that the upper portion of the stable door — which for as long as I can remember wouldn't open on its own thanks to a jammed latch — is ajar and I automatically reach out to push it open.

"Whoa!" Gus grabs my wrist. "Very wet paint! Allow me." He lets go to nudge the metal plate of the latch, and despite the warmth of the summer night my skin feels cool where I've lost contact with him.

It should be dark inside. I shouldn't be able to see anything. After all, the night's pressing in tighter by the moment, and the woodlot grows right up to the back windows of the shack, and it was the inherent darkness of the paneling that made my dad install the hideous fluorescent box lights which stripped any remaining charm from the building's interior.

But ... instead of dim gloom, my impression is of a pearly radiance. That, somehow, the building has captured the last bit of the day's light and is holding it in.

I turn to Gus. "What ...?" I know I sound clueless, but that's how I feel.

He uses the latch to open the bottom part of the door — again avoiding the wet paint — and pushes it as far back as the top portion. "Wait one sec." He disappears inside, then calls, "OK, come on in."

As I do, he reaches up and turns the switch on a camping lantern hanging at head height and the space around me jumps into view — all warm white walls and swept-clean floors. Feeling bigger than I've ever seen it, yet still cozy.

I was right that there was only so much he could do in the time I was in Toronto, but I was wrong that he couldn't transform this place.

He's done all the right things to make the biggest difference in the shortest space of time.

I make one long, slow three-sixty turn. With the walls plain, and clean, and white, the good bones of the building stand out. The wood trim around the windows. The beams, which I can notice now that the terrible fluorescents bolted to them aren't turned on.

I take another complete turn and by the time I finish it I'm blinking hard and biting my lip.

"Is it OK?" Gus asks. "Will it work for your photos?"

I take a long breath in through my nose. Concentrate on holding my voice steady. "It'll do."

"It'll do?" Gus lifts a hand to his face, rubs his forehead. There are flecks of pearly paint in his hair and there's a slash across his knuckle. "It'll do," he repeats. "It'll do."

I'm joking, I want to say. Except that's not quite right. More like, *I'm covering*. Shoving my feelings down, hard. Trying to avoid a full-on descent into lip-quivering, voice-quavering emotion.

Whatever it is, it's not fair to Gus who, paint-covered and hopeful, brought me to see the near-miracle he's worked. A huge step toward the possible salvation of the farm, achieved through the sweat and grind of the single person standing in front of me.

Get over yourself. Be the bigger person. For once in your life be gracious.

Before I can start, he reaches up and turns off the lantern. "I should have known. I should have listened to Aggie."

I want to be gracious. I would have been gracious — really, I would have — but this latest example of Aggie slagging me off behind my back really is the limit.

"Oh, sweet sugar shacks!" Instead of making me feel better, the sanitized curse just stokes my frustration. "What does Aggie want from me? I'm hustling my butt to bring in money, I sent my mother to Vancouver, and I don't even swear properly anymore out of respect for her precious children!" (my precious nieces and nephews, too, but admitting that would weaken my argument).

"Aggie ..." Gus starts.

"Oh no ..." I'm shaking my head.

"She ..."

"Don't you dare ..." If he defends her, I'll leave gracious so far in my rear-view mirror I'll never come back to it.

Gus opens his mouth, I lift my hand to keep him quiet, and he yells, "Listen to me!"

"Listen to what? Listen to you stick up for my stuck-up sister-in-law? Listen to how one more person has joined the I-hate-Hazel club? Listen to ..."

"Oh sweet sugar shacks, Hazel! Listen to me say that Aggie doesn't appreciate the hustle of your butt the way I do. Which would have been cute and flirty if you'd let me say it right off the bat, but the moment's passed, so now it's just sad and out of context."

I freeze. My hands go to my backside. "Is that a compliment?"

"What?"

"'The hustle of my butt' — is it good for a butt to have hustle?"

Gus stares at me. My heart hammers as I wait to see how this is going to go. Whether I've pushed him too far. Whether he has the sense of humour I need him to. "It's good for *your* butt to have hustle," he says.

Oh god that's sexy. Smoking hot, in fact. It's too dark now to see the natural wave in his hair, or his high cheekbones — one of which has a little scar cutting across it which I stole glances at all through dinner. His feet aren't bare, and neither is his chest but I'm flooded with an insistent heat pulsating from my insides out, my head is light, and my lungs can't find enough air.

This guy is light-hearted. He's funny. He's happy. He's kind. And even if I can't see his good looks now, if I get close enough I'll be able to feel them. "Sold."

"Excuse me?"

"I can't do this with somebody who takes themself too seriously."

"Can't do what?"

"Can't ..." I take a step toward him in the dark,

"... throw ..." one more and I'm right in front of him,

"... myself ..." I reach for his hands, and pulling them toward me, carefully place one on each of my butt cheeks,

"... at you."

"Oh," he says.

"Oh? I put your hands on my butt and you say, 'oh'?"

He shrugs. "It'll do."

It bubbles through me. Something I haven't felt for a long time. Something light and loose. It's been so long since I've been with a guy who's easy like this.

It's been, realistically, never. It's another thing I always envied about Aggie. She had my brother and he was light, and easy, and fun.

It's also been so long since I was with anybody at all, so while I start by laughing, that ends quickly when I move my mouth to Gus's.

Or next to it, anyway. It's really gotten quite dark. My lips hit stubble, and I mumble, "Whoops."

Now *he* laughs, the sound rumbling into my ear, along the sensitive nerves in my neck, spreading through my body, making me want to touch him everywhere.

"Grab me," I say.

"Like this?" With hands still on my backside he pulls me tight.

"Oh, yes ... oh, no ... wait ..." I push back a bit, reach down and grab his thigh, pulling it forward, straddling it with my own legs. "Mmm ... yes. Much better."

"Just take what you want."

"I will. Don't worry." I tighten my riding-toned inner thighs around his cargo shorts. "Feels. So. Good."

His lips have found mine now, and we're both breathing hard. Between kisses he says. "You are ..." *kiss* "... so weird ..." *nibble* "... and so hot ..."

I push my mouth hard against his. Later, my lips will hurt and the skin around them will be sore from his five o'clock shadow, but right now I don't care. Right now it would take a lot more than a little beard burn to make me stop. Like a shock from a cattle prod. Or a herd of stampeding horses.

He leans away from me, making space to lift one of his hands to the front of my shirt, cupping my breast, swiping his thumb across the swell of it. His calloused skin pulls at the thin fabric. "Sorry."

"No," I shake my head, as I reach for the hem of my shirt, haul it over my head. "Don't be sorry. Let me get that out of the way for you."

Now, with almost nothing between his work-roughened thumb and my own skin, I lean into his touch.

He takes a step back, and still gripping his leg I move with him. Or, try to. Hobbled, he overbalances, falling backward with me landing on top of him.

I'm giddy with lust and laughter. I feel simultaneously so full of adrenaline that I could do anything, and so overcome with desire that my legs might not hold me if I decided to stand up.

Better not try, then. I reach for his belt, then pause, find the glint of his eyes in the dark. "Is this OK? Since I have you overpowered, and all?"

"It would be — I definitely want it to be — except ..."

I freeze. "Are you trying to be funny again? Because this is not the time ... *oh* ..."

He's holding both hands right in front of me, where I can see them even in the near-dark, and opens them as wide as he can, palms up: *I got nothing.*

I don't either.

I throw my head back, stare at the shadowy ceiling, then find his eyes again. "Well, you know what they say — when life gives you lemons ..."

"Are we talking about lemons here? Because *I* wasn't talking about lemons."

I lean down, put my lips next to his ear, suck his ear lobe into my mouth, then release it to whisper, "Well, what I was actually talking about was making lemonade. If you're game, that is."

"Lemonade." He nods. "Now that you mention it, I actually quite like lemonade."

"In that case ..." I move down his body, and the next thing I take into my mouth isn't his ear lobe.

***

As Gus and I walk back to the farmhouse through the thick night air, my limbs are loose, muscles well-used-and-now-relaxed. Just like after a long run ... except I expect I'm going to find bruises on my knees in the morning which isn't a normal side-effect of my runs.

The temperature is perfect, with just enough breeze to keep the mosquitos away, and we get constant glimpses of the sky thick with stars, with the glowing full moon as a focal point. When the farmhouse comes into view, it too looks enchanting — lit from within by the lights of family life, with the darkness masking the crumbling brickwork of the chimney, curling edges of the shingles, and paint-peeling fascia.

That feeling again — it twines around my ribs, tugs at my heart, as I remember coming along this very path, dirt hard-packed under the soles of my paddock boots, knowing the horses were taken care of behind me, hearing my parents' voices mingling with the neighbours' as they had drinks on the porch, seeing Aggie's bike leaning against the porch and knowing she and Brody would be taking advantage of the empty house to do more kissing than watching as they sat in front of a movie.

Until now I've been leaning into these nostalgic moments — after all, they drew me 4,500 kilometres across the country — but there's a problem this time. Because the bittersweet ache pulsing through me right now, reminds me almost exactly of that feeling that stopped me in my tracks earlier this evening — the one I identified as loneliness.

I'm not ready to think about that right now.

Besides, there's something else I don't want to think about niggling at me.

My goodnight with Gus.

I really don't want it to be mushy or sentimental. I also don't want it to be awkward. Not drawn-out.

I don't want it to be something our encounter wasn't, which was lots of fun, mutually satisfying, no strings attached, and between consenting adults.

Perfect.

Exactly what I needed after the definitely not-fun relationship I've just fled from.

The walk so far has been quiet and companionable. When not fighting nostalgia, I've been replaying this thing he did with his baby finger — *Was that planned? Was it a happy accident? Why did it feel so good?*

Now, though, his truck is in sight and it's clear we're going to have to part ways, and I catch my shoulders lifting toward my ears, my teeth clenching, and my hands forming tight fists.

I'm running through all the cringey things he might do so I can be prepared.

If he tries to kiss me, I'll offer him my cheek.

If he asks when we can see each other again, I'll smile and say we'll both be at the next festival meeting.

If he says, "That was really special," or "I think we had a great connection," or "I wish this night didn't have to end," I'll be firm and clear — "It was *fun*." Fun is the important word.

"Whoo-hoo!!! Gus! Auntie Hazel!" The screen door swings all the way back and hits the wall, and Violet, Ali, and Patrick all appear pyjamaed, barefoot, and adorable on the front porch with Violet talking a mile a minute. "You missed milkshakes! Dad made them with Moose Tracks ice cream *and* we were allowed to put whipped cream on top —"

"— and chocolate sprinkles —" Patrick pipes up.

"Don't interrupt!"

"Don't tell everything, I get to tell some, too."

"I'm older."

"Yeah, and bossier ..."

Meanwhile Ali steps between them, holding out a big glass covered in condensation and various sticky, sugary looking drips. "There's one for you."

"Ali!" Both her siblings stop yelling at each other to yell at her and she shrugs. "It was melting while you two were fighting."

"Why thank-you ma'am." Gus steps forward and takes it from her. "Don't mind if I do."

With two big gulps about half of it's gone. "Mm-mm. Dee-licious!"

All the kids giggle, their animosity to each other overcome by their adoration of Gus.

He is rather adorable — with a chocolate mustache overarching his upper lip and a boop of whipped cream on the end of his nose. It would be fun to lick those off. *Next time ...*

Then I remind myself I was prepared to tell him "next time" is the next regularly scheduled festival meeting.

Well, I suppose if he asks we could figure out another time for a just-for-fun, doesn't-have-to-mean-anything get-together.

And I could bring whipped cream.

"... Auntie Hazel?"

"Huh?" I blink my eyes into focus so I can meet Ali's gaze. "Sorry, honey. I was thinking of something else."

"I was asking if you want some before Gus drinks it all."

"I, oh ..." As I turn to Gus he's already shaking his head. "Oh, sweetie, your Auntie Hazel doesn't want to share with me — she might get my germs. Right, Hazel?"

I stare at the lips I was kissing ten minutes ago. I lift my hand to the skin around my mouth rubbed tender by his stubble.

Before I can answer he winks at me, hands the glass back to my niece, and says, "Thank you, kids for that delicious milkshake."

He turns to me and kisses me on the cheek. "Thank you, Hazel, for a fun evening."

Then he gets in his truck and drives away.

He kissed me on the cheek. He said it was fun.

That's what I wanted. Good. Great. No clinginess. No misunderstandings.

The trees by the trailer block my view of his taillights and I turn back to my chattering nieces and nephew.

All three of them are trying to get back into the house at the same time. They jostle, and hip-bump, and step on each other's toes, saying, "move!" "no, you move!" "I was here first!"

Then like a great clog of leaves suddenly clearing a gutter, they all tumble inside at the same time, squawking and giggling, and I'm left outside in the quiet yard, looking into the illuminated house.

***

I've got the Gimme Shelter folder open in front of me when I hear the creak of the trailer stairs.

The sensor triggers the small solar-powered light over the door, spotlighting my sister-in-law's face.

"M'in."

She points to the toothbrush sticking out of my mouth. "Do you always welcome visitors while you're brushing your teeth?"

"M r'ding 'ntracts."

"You're reading contracts. While brushing your teeth." She nods. "Of course. Everybody does that."

I sigh, which sprays a bit of toothpaste across the page open in front of me, so I go to the bathroom, rinse out my mouth, and call through the open door. "I'm multi-tasking."

"Right." The look Aggie gives me makes me feel like she can see right into my brain. To the turmoil that won't let me settle, driving me to simultaneously get ready for bed, and also do something productive in case I can't sleep. She shrugs. "Whatever. I shouldn't judge. I told Brody I was coming here because you forgot this —" she holds out the reusable shopping bag Violet used to carry the gifts she brought her siblings "— but I was mostly trying to avoid the multi-tasking required to get three moose-track-milkshaked kids to bed at the same time."

I take the bag. "Thanks. Goodnight."

Aggie lifts her eyebrows. "I'm pretty sure they won't be in bed just yet. You can show me the photos of the sugar shack to help pass the time."

Photos. Not only did I forget to take them, I forgot they were the whole point of my after-dinner walk to the sugar shack.

"Umm ... by the time I got there it was too dark to take any."

Now Aggie knits her eyebrows. "But I thought that was the whole point of going at that time of night. To get photos in the evening light like this." She holds out her phone to show me a truly stunning shot of the sugar shack with all its imperfections blurred by shadows and its best features highlighted by the last golden rays of the sun.

Gus must have taken it right before I got there. I'm pissed off at him for sending her the picture and I'm pissed off at her for pressing me with it. I wish I hadn't gotten rid of my toothbrush — I'd like an excuse not to talk to her right now.

"Yeah, well Gus took that one because my phone battery died on the drive home from Toronto."

"Is that right?"

I nod. "That's right. That's why I got that phone call on the landline at your place. They tried to call my cell and it was shut off."

"Hmm ... yes, the phone call. That's a whole other thing I'm going to make you tell me about later, but for now let's talk about how you didn't even try to take photographs. You just shagged Gus."

"What?!" Here I thought Gus was too nice. "Did he send you a photo of the sugar shack captioned 'I just got naked with your sister-in-law here?'"

"Oh. My. God," she says. "You really did."

"I didn't *shag* him!" I'm fully aware I'm not handling this well. My cheeks are going hot, which makes me scared the beard rash is going to stand out. I have to get a grip on this. I have to figure out what she knows, and take it back a step. Or several. "So, he didn't say anything?"

"Of course he didn't," Aggie says. "He didn't need to." She reaches for my left side and grabs something. I look down. It's the fabric care tag sewn into the seam of my t-shirt. The one that should be on the inside.

"Shucks," I start, then make a deliberate hard turn to "Shit!" What a classic screw-up. "Do you think the kids noticed?"

She shakes her head. "It was pretty dark. Plus, as far as they're concerned, you walk on water — if they did notice, they'd just want to wear their shirts inside-out, too."

As far as they're concerned. Her tone suggests their judgment is suspect.

"Speaking of which," she continues. "They also worship Gus. With good reason." There's a warning tone in her voice.

"Meaning?" I prompt.

"Meaning, don't break his heart."

My heart twinges. I should tell her how he breezed away without a backward glance.

Wait, no, what I *should* tell her is to stop throwing shade at me.

I'm not *that* bad. Or, even if I am, talking about me behind my back makes her just as bad.

We're way past three strikes, Aggies's had at least half-a-dozen. I should have it out with her.

On the other hand, I'm tired. I'm not convinced I have the energy required to do justice to my argument. I really don't want Aggie to get the better of me.

"Mo-o-om!" A voice floating through the still night air decides it. Telling off my sister-in-law will have to wait when there are munchkins up way past their bedtimes.

I sit in the empty trailer and stare at the door Aggie just left through.

I thought I'd feel good about today. I drove all the way to Toronto and back, and showed my niece a good time in the process. I secured funding from Trent, both for the Gimme Shelter festival, and for the farm.

I had the closest thing to sex I've had in a long time. And it was good.

It all feels empty, though. Toronto always leaves me feeling a mix of exhilaration and grime. Trent has my back, but he lives in the aforementioned grimy city. Violet is fantastic, but she's in her bedroom at the farmhouse and I'm all alone here. The romp in the sugar shack — well, somehow instead of a lingering satisfaction, I'm feeling an expanding void. Better not to think too hard about that one. And why bother, because my undeniably biggest mess-up was not even getting the photos I need to clinch the film shoot.

Stupid.

The worst part is, Aggie was right. That magical, forgiving, transformative evening light was perfect.

I guess I'll have to set my alarm extra early in the hopes the morning light will have a similar effect.

I reach for my phone to Google when, exactly, dawn is, then schedule my wake up accordingly, when I see a new notification.

An email.

From Gus.

Hope these work for you it says, followed by a selection of photos as good or better than the one Aggie showed me. Interior and exterior shots all with that same dreamy feel. No filter could produce this effect, but one that tried would have to be named "idyll" or "romance" or, possibly ... "nostalgia."

That's it, exactly. Gus may not have bottled nostalgia, but he's lit, and painted, and photographed it, then handed it to me to sell to Trent and the film crew clients.

It might just be a longing for the past that assures the farm's future.

I send the photos off to Trent exactly as Gus sent them, then I hit reply to Gus's message. **They're perfect. Thank you.**

I toy with trying to add something flirty. Or dirty. Or even cute. Then I think of Aggie's opinion that Gus is too nice for me. I think of how casually Gus left me this evening and realize he probably also knows he's too nice for me.

I hit send and crawl into bed and as I lie listening to all the old farm sounds — the breeze rustling the aspen leaves, the distant bark of the neighbour's dog, and the sawing of a particularly loud cricket under my open window, I think it would be easier if I still believed the gnawing ache in my gut was nostalgia.

Eleven

MY PHONE WAKES ME UP, buzzing and jittering its way across the tiny kitchen counter.

I groan. Even several days in, I'm still finding the thin mattress ridiculously comfortable, and last night the temperature got down to a heavenly — and very sleeping-friendly — ten degrees, and *why didn't I remember to turn my notifications off?* I normally do, so I don't have to deal with endless questions from (boss), or last-minute (and completely avoidable) emergencies from clients, or complaints from Tom.

Yesterday, though, I wanted Aggie to be able to reach me in case something happened with Patrick. It felt different to actually *want* somebody to be able to call me.

Something else feels different this morning.

I blink a few times, and let my short-term memory stir to life and realize these notifications might be about good things.

Trent could be emailing details about the film crew contract, or the festival funding, or both.

Violet could be texting me about the riding lesson I'm supposed to give my nieces and nephew today.

Gus could be reaching out to say ... I sigh. I do completely recognize my own hypocrisy at being prepared to despise him for any sign of clinginess last night, while this morning I cling to the hope of a message from him.

I despise myself for it, too. Despise myself for caring. Recognize how unattractive it is to want someone, not for who they are, but because they might want me.

Despicable, unattractive, hypocritical me.

Well, rather than dwell on that, I think I'll just check my phone.

What do they say? Two out of three ain't bad?

Trent: **That place is amazing. The client replied two minutes after I sent the photos. It's a yes — you'll have the contract by end of day.**

Violet: **Auntie Hazel, my mom says afternoon will be best for our lesson. I told her it might be too hot for the horses, but she said we have to go to the dentist this morning. *Please* say we can still ride!**

There are more messages, but one is from my mother, and the one after it is from Tom and those revive the familiar feeling that nothing good can come from checking my messages, so I put down my phone and pull on my running shoes.

I have a lot of thinking to do, and the best way to do it is on the move.

It's not that I'm complaining about my run — my runs are pretty much the one thing in life I've never complained about — but it is noticeable that my ponytail sticks to the back of my neck on each back-and-forth swing, and the seam of my tank top has chafed the soft skin of my inner arm — both sure signs that I'm sweatier today than I was when I ran yesterday.

Those, and the endless licking Milford's subjecting me to.

I finished my run with a slow lap around the farm and because the horses were grazing near the gate, I decided to lean on the top rail to plan this afternoon's riding lesson out with the inspiration for it right in front of me.

At first, I think Milford's sweet. "Aren't you a lovely little man?" I reach my hand out and he licks my fingers and I melt a little inside, telling the others — "See? It wouldn't kill you to lift your greedy heads up and say hi."

To be fair, even though he's the farthest away, Quin does come and give me a soft bump with his nose, before dropping it to the grass again. Cressy grazes on as though I don't exist. Banks gives me full-on side-eye, complete with a generous view of the white ring around the edge of his eye, which makes him look particularly dangerous. I'm sure it's not my imagination that he redoubles the ferocity of his tearing at the grass.

Meanwhile, Milford redoubles the ferocity of his licking. Up my forearms, then past my elbows.

"OK, buddy. That's enough."

He doesn't even pause, just tips his head to the side so he can reach my neck. "Um, ick. No." I shove at his head, and he shoves back.

"Is he always like this?" I ask the others. Both Quin and Cressy flick one ear in my direction as though confirming, yes — the aggressive grooming is a thing, and they're just going to keep quiet and let me be Milford's victim this time. Banks, however, snorts.

It's dangerous to anthropomorphize animals. I learned that way back when I was working with the auction ponies, and it's something I've never forgotten. Horses are horses — not human souls living in stronger, faster, more elegant bodies than ours. There are really only a few things you need to know about horses.

- They're not violent but they can kill you.

- They're herd animals, and the rules of the herd are far more important than rules imposed by humans.

- Most of their decisions are motivated by food and / or fear.

This knowledge has served me well. It's kept me from being bitten by getting between a particularly ravenous horse and his sweetfeed, and it's helped me to get dozens of horses to do what I want them to by simply removing fear from the equation.

"You're some kind of horse whisperer," a woman told me when I loose-reined her mount — legendary for running out, refusing, and just generally stopping at everything presented to him — clear around an eight-jump course.

"Nope." I shook my head. "I just took away his fear of being reefed in the mouth."

She wasn't happy, but nobody ever called me a middle-aged-woman whisperer — and at least she had a horse who jumped.

As Bank gives another snort, followed by a little head shake that tumbles his forelock over his eye and elevates his side-eye from scorn to full-on eff-you territory, all my horse common-sense flees me. Instead of perceiving the gelding as simply enjoying his grazing, and wanting to make sure I'm not going to try to stop him, as well as possibly being in need of a forelock trim, I see him as taunting me. Mocking me because I can't even manage to make a very small pony stop licking me.

"That's it," I say. "We'll see what I can manage."

I yank my arm away from Milford's tongue, duck through the fence, and reach Banks' side in two quick strides. Clearly he's used to Violet's timidity and Marta's incompetence, because he's just lifting his head with an expression I read as surprised (more anthropomorphizing) when I take hold of a tuft of mane at the base of his withers and use skills I learned at a long-ago vaulting clinic, to spring onto his back.

He may have been too slow to stop me from mounting, but there's nothing sluggish about the way he reacts once I'm up. He rocks back onto his haunches, then springs forward in a halt-to-canter transition I'd die to get in a dressage test.

He accelerates through canter to a hand gallop with a speed that has me cursing my impulsivity, wishing I was wearing a helmet, and wondering what on earth I was trying to prove.

He's so fast. He sweeps around the open grassy area of the field without slackening his pace and as he does, my fear recedes. His stride is smooth and balanced. He doesn't lean, and I'm able to close my hip angle and follow the fast three beats. It's those very three beats that tell me this horse isn't running away — he hasn't even moved into a full gallop — he's just running fast and having fun.

As we sail back past the gate, Milford and Quin, who have been watching with pricked ears, join in as well, first taking a few hesitant trot steps, then accelerating into their own forward runs.

Even with his newly acquired entourage, Banks doesn't buck, or even hurtle forward. He just keeps going, hooves thrumming, ears forward, nostrils flared.

When we pass the gate again, the two older gentlemen drop off, rejoining Cressy who never gave up her grazing.

I lay my hand flat against Banks' neck. He keeps moving, but flicks on ear back to me.

I straighten on his back and tighten my inner thighs.

The hand gallop transitions to a canter.

"Whoa," I say.

He shakes his head and flows to a forward, long-striding trot which, thankfully for the sake of my delicate bits, he doesn't stay in for long.

As he walks back to the gate, neck long, head low, and easy walk swaying my hips, I'm thinking about the upcoming riding lesson I'm giving the kids. I may not have made a traditional lesson plan, but I've figured out something important.

Banks isn't mean. He isn't nasty. He isn't a runaway. But there's also no way my timid niece should be riding him.

There's nobody around when I walk by the house, but there is coffee brewed. The aroma hangs sharp in the soft summer air of the morning.

It reaches out, curls into my nostrils, and gives a tug which definitely isn't the lust I felt for Gus last night, but

is a baby-sized approximation. The message is clear —
my body wants the coffee.

Two minutes later I'm settled on the top step, leaning
against the porch railing giving my body what it asked
for. Two things it asked for, actually, since there was also
a tray of warm-from-the-oven poppyseed muffins on the
stovetop.

Creaking stairs, scuffing feet, the whine then slam of
the screen porch and I'm surrounded by children. One
second later, I'm not so tightly surrounded anymore as
they all take one step back.

"Aunt Hazel, you don't smell the best." Note to self —
if ever dressing up for a big event, get Patrick to check my
rear view. He's cut-to-the-quick honest.

Ali wrinkles her nose. "You don't look the best, either."

Violet gasps. "Ali! You know we don't talk about
people's appearance!"

I laugh. "It's OK, Violet. They're both right. I've run
eight kilometres this morning, then I had a little
bareback ride."

"Oh." She points to the line of dirt along my inner legs.
"Is that why you have that mark?"

I nod. "Since Marta left, I think those horses aren't
quite getting the grooming they used to." I rub at a
section of the grime and it peels away under my finger,
leaving a clean-looking break in the band of filth.

"Did you ride Quin?" Violet asks.

Ali snorts. "Of course she rode Quin! Her knees would drag on the ground if she rode Cressy or Milford, and nobody would be crazy enough to ride Banks bareback."

Patrick's eyebrows shoot up. "She better not have ridden Milford." My nephew and I are on fairly friendly terms, but that doesn't extend to him wanting to let me ride his horse.

"We'll talk about horses this afternoon at our lesson."

"OK," Violet says. "But I still don't think Ali should have said that about how you look."

"I know what you mean, Violet, and I'd usually agree with you, but here's a rule I've heard that I think is pretty good — you should only comment on how somebody looks if they can change it in a minute or two."

"What do you mean?"

"You give me some examples. What can't somebody change about how they look in a minute or two?"

"How tall they are!" Patrick yells.

Ali twirls her own hair that tumbles halfway down her back. "How long their hair is ..."

Patrick snorts. "What if they put it in a ponytail and cut it all off with one snip?"

Ali's face goes white and she gathers her hair in close against her neck. "Nobody would do that."

God. Great. Now I've made my niece afraid somebody's going to cut all her hair off. Even when I try to make people feel good, I fail miserably. I should just stop talking.

"They would if they were donating it to make wigs for people with cancer," Patrick pushes.

I hold up my hand. "Even then, people who do that plan it for a long time, so we'll take Ali's answer and move on."

"If they still have their baby teeth." Violet reaches up and gives one tooth a wiggle and my heart breaks for my sweet little niece. I'd like to believe little girls wouldn't tease one another about having baby teeth, but I don't. I know what those girls are like when they grow up. *Please let that tooth fall out before school starts again*, I think.

"What about things people can change really quickly and easily?" I ask.

Patrick jumps up and down. "Oh! Oh! Oh! If their fly is down!"

"Yeah," Ali says. "Because yours always is."

"Not *always*. And anyway, yours used to be, before you started wearing skirts."

Ali puts her hands on her hips. "Which is not something I can change about myself, so you're not supposed to mention it."

This seems like an opportunity to end the conversation somewhere near the point I was trying to make in the first place, so I seize it. "Exactly! Ali's right. She is who she is and she shouldn't want to, or need to change that, and nobody should comment on it. Whereas, if I had a poppyseed stuck in my teeth from your mom's super-delicious muffin I just ate, I'd be able to change that really fast, and I'd actually *want* you to tell me."

"In that case Auntie Hazel ..."

"Yes, Violet, what is it? Do I have a poppyseed stuck in my teeth?"

"No ... or actually, let me see —" She leans in close and inspects my mouth. "No poppyseed, but I guess what Patrick and Ali said is true — you're not completely your best self at the moment, and you could change that in just a few minutes by having a shower."

I laugh. "Yes. You're absolutely right." I hold my empty mug out to her. If you'll take this inside, I'll head straight to the trailer for my shower."

She takes the mug and adds, "Also, just because you don't have a poppyseed in your teeth, I think you should still make sure to brush your teeth, because your breath does smell a bit like coffee." She wrinkles her nose. "Sorry, was that OK to say?"

"Yes." I nod. "Absolutely." I walk toward the trailer with my hand cupped over my mouth. Sure enough, coffee breath.

Nothing like a trio of tweens to put you in your place.

Twelve

I SMELL GOOD. I look good. Good enough, anyway. Good enough to tour all the festival sites where I just-maybe-possibly could run into Gus.

I stop at Quinte County Coffee and get them to fill a Thermos with steaming fair trade coffee, and fold a box around a selection of home-baked organic baked goods, then I head to the community hall.

It looks like a command centre. I suppose it is a command centre. There's a low-tech station with a table covered with stacks of poster board and a bowl of Sharpies, along with every kind of tape and twine you could imagine. A pile of stakes lies on the floor. Brenda catches me eyeing everything up. "Sign-making station. It's a win-win. Parents drop their kids off here to make signs while they run errands in town, and we get a bunch of signs to use at the festival."

She points to the corner where there's a stack of poster-boarded signs. The one on top declares **Port-a-Potties This Way** and is illustrated with a fat rainbow-coloured arrow. "We end up with a lot of directions to the toilets." She pulls a lollipop out of her pocket. "We use these to bribe them to make more boring signs about entrances and exits and food kiosks."

I lift my offerings toward her. "Speaking of bribery — coffee? Baked goods?"

She hesitates, then smiles. "Sure. I normally bring my own, but a coffee from Quinte County is a real treat. Thank you."

I bite back a smile because the entire Thermos of coffee cost the same amount as two single cups at my regular coffee shop back in the city. Another thing I won't miss about not going back.

Wait. Am I not going back? Really? Like not at all? When did I decide that?

"Hazel?"

I snap back to Brenda. "Sorry, I was a million miles away." *Or, more precisely, forty-three-hundred kilometres.* "What did you say?"

"I wondered if you've finished going through Iris's books yet?" She sighs. "We don't want to face it, but unless you can tell us something completely unexpected — which, don't get me wrong, nobody's a miracle-worker and Iris was a very bad financial manager — we've been saying we should probably build some messaging into the festival about this being the last year." She bites her lip. "Who knows — it might even prompt people to donate a little more than they usually would. We can go out with a bang."

It's tempting to blurt out, "Hey, no worries! The festival is saved!" but Trent promised me paperwork later today, and both a healthy superstition and a strongly developed business sense tell me not to blab until I've seen the details in writing.

Plus, it would be wrong to tell one person without telling the others. Especially Gus, since he was the one who pulled me into this festival.

Yeah, that's why.

"Well," I say. "It sounds like something we should meet to discuss. Can you come to the farm around 6:00? I'll order in pizza."

"We don't have the budget for pizza."

"I'll see what I can do about the pizza, if you can make it."

Brenda nods. "You're right. We should meet. I'll be there."

"Great. I want to invite the others, too, and bring them coffee before it goes cold. Since you're the nerve centre here, can you tell me where I'll find them all?"

"Peace and Kumar will be at the community grounds. We usually lose track of Flora, but this year I got her to install Find my Friend on her phone so ... yup, there she is. At the start of the ninth line heading south. The parade route goes all the way to Mainline Road, so if you leave now, you should be able to catch her partway along. And Gus ..." She wrinkles her nose. "I thought I would have seen him by now. I was expecting him to drop off some supplies this morning. You can wait for him if you want, but you might miss Flora."

"No, that's fine. I'll head out to find her now. Maybe you can tell Gus that's where I've gone? And mention the meeting at the farm tonight?"

The door opens and I whirl around, breath held, heart hammering. When a woman files in with two kids in tow, I breathe again. She's fanning herself. "Lordy Brenda, it's already stoking up out there. Can you order a cooler day for the festival?" She laughs at her own joke as she directs the children to the sign-making station.

Brenda's already on her way to the table. "We could really use some signs for the parking area, kids ..."

"Brenda?" I prompt.

"Hmm, yes. See you at six o'clock."

"Gus?"

"Yes, Gus — I'll tell him, or ask him ... no, honey, you can't put a toilet on your sign ..."

Brenda may be one of the most accomplished people I've ever met, and I one-hundred percent believe if she puts her mind to anything to do with the festival, she'll make it happen, but as I step out of the semi-air-conditioned hall into the full-on furnace-blast of the morning heat, I have almost no faith that Gus will show up at the farm this evening if I leave it solely to Brenda to invite him.

Another frazzled-looking mother is on her way into the hall with one little girl running in front of her yelling, "I want to make a sign for the toilets!" and another dragging behind. The lagging child is staring at my car. "Is that your car?"

"Yes."

"I like it. Our car is boring."

Her mother gives me quick smile. "We just spent a very hot few minutes walking in circles at the grocery store parking lot because we couldn't find where we parked our truck." She points to a grey pickup that looks like every second truck on the road around here. "That would never happen with your little car."

"No it wouldn't." I slide into the driver's seat and think at least if Brenda remembers to point Gus in the direction I'm heading he shouldn't have any trouble spotting me in my bright car.

**

As promised, I find Flora on the ninth line, halfway between Main Street in town and Mainline Road. She's standing in the middle of the road, staring at a driveway.

I leave my flashy car on the side of the road where it will be visible for a good, long distance, and join her.

"You can't really see it, can you?"

I stare at the leafy forest growing close in on both sides of the driveway. Truth be told, you can barely see the driveway. If Flora hadn't been stopped here, I would have coasted right by. "See what, exactly?"

"Ah! I was right. You can't see it at all!" She strides forward, grabs a huge branch, and yanks it sideways.

I blink, squint, tilt my head. "Is that a wall?"

"It's a school bus shelter. Number seventeen on the tour."

I snort. "I don't think so."

Flora steps back, puts her hands on her hips. "Exactly." She lifts her phone and snaps a shot. "There's the before." She strides over to her SUV parked on the side of the road, reaches into the open hatch, and pulls out a saw.

"What are you ...?"

She shakes her head. "Not *me*." She pulls out another saw. "*Us*. Come on — you start from the left, I'll start from the right, saw any branch growing in front of the shelter. It'll take five minutes."

You don't have to take the saw, I think. *You don't have to hack a bus shelter out of what's basically a jungle. This is above and beyond.*

Which is all true, except even as I'm thinking this, Flora, forty years my senior has stepped off the road and into the bush and is sawing vigorously at the branch she already showed me. The sound of a car sends me whirling around. It's not Gus's pickup, though. It's a sedan, and the middle-aged driver stares at Flora working like a Trojan, then back at me, watching her.

"You're younger than her," I call after it. "Why don't you get out and saw?" But I've already picked up my saw and stepped through a gap in the dense vegetation.

***

Fifteen minutes later there's an impressive pile of boughs on the side of the road.

There's sweat trickling down my back and when I lift my hand to rub at my cheek, it comes away with blood on it, courtesy of a close encounter with a sharp branch. Flora, with not one of her neat, carefully cut silver hairs out of place, reaches out and pulls a leafy twig from my hair. "Just as well we were working in the shade. Otherwise it would have been hot work."

I pull my shirt away from my sticky skin. "Oh yeah. It sure would have been."

So much for five minutes' worth of work. While it's true the bus shelter is now visible, it still looks terrible. And my efforts to both look and smell good in case I run into Gus are pretty much back to square one. If Patrick and Ali were here, they'd have some hard truths to tell me. Which wouldn't strictly be fair since, with zero shower access, my current state isn't something I can change in a couple of minutes.

I brace myself to say no when Flora suggests we pick up paint and rollers but she just takes my saw, puts it back in her SUV along with hers, brushes her hands together and says, "That'll do. I'll send Milly Tidvale a photo of this, then I'll send her a photo of Jessie Locke's shelter over on the twelfth line —" Flora shows me a picture of a tidy bus shelter made up mostly of sparkling clean windows adorned with overflowing flower boxes, "— and she'll have this shelter spic and span in time for the parade even if she has to drive out from Toronto to do it herself. You see, back in grade school Jessie beat out Milly to win the regional spelling bee ... on a technicality. Or, at least, Milly says it was a technicality." She laughs. "Some people say those two will kill each other with their competitiveness, but I find it can be quite useful."

Flora would slay in my old job. I consider telling her so but instead offer, "Coffee?"

"Oh no, dear. I don't need caffeine to boost my energy levels. I do just fine on my own."

She blinks twice then furrows her eyebrows. "I hope that isn't why you came all the way out here — to offer me coffee."

"No. I was talking to Brenda. She said you've all been discussing the festival's demise."

"Hmm. Yes, well, don't take it personally. I'm sure you're very good at your job back in Vancouver, but Iris really was a terrible manager, and of course it's not like you're here long term. It wasn't fair of Gus to involve you."

I open my mouth to ask if she, by any chance, has seen Gus today, when she says, "Of course Peace is an addict."

"Excuse me?"

"She can't get enough coffee."

"Coffee. Right. Of course." Honestly, I'm glad Flora didn't accept any — I'm having a hard enough time keeping up with her in an uncaffeinated state. "I was planning to see Peace next, so that's good to know."

"Yes, and Kumar will eat most of those baked goods — he loves his food."

"Speaking of food, I've already told Brenda that I'm hoping you can all come to the farm at six o'clock for a meeting over pizza." I hesitate. "If you eat pizza, that is."

"Food of the gods!" Flora says. "As long as you don't get it from Jo-Jo's, that is. He also owns the garage and he overcharged the last time I took my car in for service."

"Right. OK. Not Jo-Jo's." Seems like Milly and Jessie's isn't the only feud in town.

"If you see Gus, could you also mention the get-together to him?"

Flora's grabbed her saw again. "You missed a branch, dear."

"Oh, I'm sorry."

She's already walking toward it. "It's fine. I'll fix it."

"Flora?"

"Yes," she calls. "This evening at six."

"And?" I prompt.

I think she says Gus's name, but it's hard to tell over the energetic zzz-zzz of her hand sawing.

***

When I get to the community grounds, Kumar is pacing out a square with Peace standing in the middle saying:

"No, I think it should be bigger."

"Not that big — I think you should make it smaller."

"Hmm ... I think that might be too small."

Although I'd probably want to kill Peace if I was Kumar — even just watching makes me want to snap at her — he's all good humour, starting over, trying again.

"Coffee?" I offer Peace as a way of diverting her attention from Kumar.

"Baked goods?" I offer him as a reward for putting up with her.

As Flora predicted, they each eagerly accept my offerings. And, as I intended, there's tranquility as Peace sips her steaming drink and Kumar slowly and steadily eats his way through a muffin, then a danish, then a donut.

"Since you're here," Peace says, "Tell me what you think of this idea." Kumar starts shaking his head. "I know you don't like it," she tells him. "But it's practical."

"What's practical?" I ask. "What idea?"

"Given that we already hold an auction for the built-on-site bus shelters, I think we should also auction off the festival's equipment — our tents, and tables — pretty much all the stuff we have to store. If this is the last festival, we should be raising as much money as we can."

Kumar's head-shaking has gotten even more vehement. "It's irresponsible to sell off the festival assets — what will happen if somebody finds a way to run it next year, or the year after."

"It's irresponsible to keep all those things and — what? — store them somewhere? How's that going to work? Who will pay for that?"

"Whoa!" I say.

They both turn to me and, at the same time, both say, "You agree with me, right?"

"Do I have to agree with anyone?"

Again they chorus, "Yes!"

"I mean, do I have to agree with anyone right now? Does this have to be decided immediately?"

"No!" Kumar says.

Peace frowns. "It does soon."

I hold up my hand. "I've already spoken to Brenda and Flora. I'd like everyone to come to a meeting at the farm tonight. I'm ordering pizza. I know there's a lot of speculation about the festival's future and we can discuss it then."

"Tonight, you say?" Peace asks.

"Pizza, you say?" Kumar asks.

"Yes," I answer to both of them. "The pizza won't be Jo-jo's," I tell Kumar. "In case that matters."

"Oh, yes," Peace says. "There was that run-in with Flora."

"Anyway, if you can come at 6:00, that would be great. And, also, if you could mention it to Gus. I thought I might see him on my travels this morning, but I haven't come across him."

Kumar pauses with a croissant halfway to his mouth. "There's no guarantee we'll see him. Why don't you just text him?"

It's no surprise Kumar is the first to ask me this. The three women volunteers are brilliant, but Kumar has something none of them has. Common sense.

"I don't actually have his number, but also it's not a formal thing, I just thought you could mention it if you saw him, you know that the group is meeting at the farm ..."

Peace cuts me off. "Six-one-three, five-five-five, one-two-three-four."

It takes me a second to realize she's reciting a phone number. Gus's, presumably.

"Oh, I guess I could enter it in my phone. Just a second."

Peace gives me a look that, if it came from a teenager, would read "duh." She's right — *duh* — I should have had Gus's number a long time ago and of course it would be very weird not to take it now.

But, as I punch it into my phone, with Kumar very kindly repeating it for me more slowly, I can't help but feel like this puts me in the driver's seat. Now I can contact Gus if I want to. In a world where my phone is full of people asking me for answers, and sending me messages I don't want to read, it was nice to have this thing with Gus be about chance encounters at the pond, or the bus shelter, or the sugar shack ...

Mmm ... the sugar shack. I've been nursing a crick in my shoulder blade all morning that I haven't minded one bit because it reminds me of a particularly intense moment when ...

"Hazel? Is that it? Do you have the number? Can I move on? Because if this is the last festival we're ever going to hold, it had better be a good one."

"Yes! Yes, I've got it. That's fine. Thank you. Please make sure to come to the farm this evening."

She's already heading off to meet a truck pulling into the grounds with a load of lumber protruding from the back. "Yes, yes ..."

Kumar waits an extra second, long enough to give me a sweet smile and say, "We'll tell Gus if we see him." Then he also hustles off to meet the driver.

As I turn to head back to my car — conspicuous in the middle of the nearly empty parking lot — a pickup truck slows on the main road with its turn signal flashing. It looks a lot like Gus's truck. The same size. The same colour.

As I watch, the signal flicks off and it accelerates past the parking entrance.

Couldn't have been Gus then. There's no way he could have missed my car.

I stop in my tracks. Think about that for a moment. *No way he could have missed it.*

Wouldn't it just be a kicker that as I'm getting more and more eager to see him, he's getting more and more eager to avoid me?

Or, it could be karma. The universe giving me what I've earned after all these years.

I suppose it's only right that I needed to be a lot nicer, a lot earlier in my life to deserve a guy like Gus.

That doesn't mean I have to like it, though.

Thirteen

SHOULD I? SHOULDN'T I?

As I walk the path to meet the kids at the barn, the two questions run through my head.

If I want to make sure Gus comes tonight, I have the means to invite him ... although if I'm right that he's trying to avoid me he could still easily wiggle out of an invitation.

I don't want him to wiggle out of it. I want him to come. More importantly, I want him to come of his own accord. I want him to *want* to come.

That feeling strikes again in the pit of my stomach. I want him to want me.

Oh lord, it really is true. I'm not nostalgic. I'm just flat-out lonely. And the loneliness monster inside me has seized on Gus. A very nice guy and completely innocent bystander seduced by the not-very-nice me scheming to fill my empty life.

Speaking of seduction — I'm walking past the sugar shack.

It looks so sweet, and charming, and marketable. I snap a photo of it snug in the leafy greenness of the

sweltering afternoon and text it to Trent. **Good call –
would you look at this place?** and I decide that's it. No more
texting. Even here under the trees the humidity is
making my skin clammy and roasting my toes in my
paddock boots. Time to get to the barn and get out on the
horses before the heat and the loneliness combine to
make me send an unguarded, or unwise message to Gus.

I need to try to keep cool, even if the weather isn't
cooperating.

***

"I expect extra good grooming!" I clap my hands as I
survey each child-horse pair. "You saw how dirty my legs
were this morning! You have to keep your standards up."

"But you were riding bareback," Patrick mumbles.

"True. But what if I said you, also, are riding bareback
this afternoon?"

"What?!?" The chorus comes from all three kids at the
same time. Patrick looks up from grooming Milford with
gleaming eyes. Ali gives me a sideways glance I don't
know how to read. From Banks's stall there's a clatter,
then a sniff, so that's where I head, ruffling Patrick's hair
as I pass. "Brush that pony."

I find Violet wiping away a tear. "Violet, honey, what's
wrong?"

She turns to me, eyes shining with many more unshed tears. As soon as her attention's off him, Banks reaches for her back pocket. "Oh, Banks!" It's the snappiest I've ever heard Violet's voice. She shoves him away with a firmness he probably needs, but which is unlike her. "How could you Auntie Hazel?"

"How could I what, Violet?"

"How could you say we're riding bareback when you know I'd love to ride bareback, and I used to when Milford was my pony, but I can't on Banks — I know *you* can, but *I* can't — so I won't get to go, which I'd almost prefer because otherwise I have to ride him with a saddle when nobody else has to and I won't even like it anyway, because *I don't like riding this horse.*"

Her last words come out with a vehemence that seems to surprise her. She immediately turns to the gelding and says, "Sorry you had to hear that. You are a very good horse, but I'm not good enough to ride you."

"I agree," I say.

She blinks. I don't know if she's surprised I'm not arguing with her, or if she thinks I'm insulting her riding.

"I don't want you to ride Banks."

"So, then what? I just don't get to go? I thought this was a lesson for all of us. I've been looking forward to it since yesterday." Her lip is quivering.

"I'd like you to ride Quin."

"Quin?"

"None other."

"But Quin is perfect. Quin is the best horse ever. Quin is ... yours."

I nod. "Didn't you just tell me Banks is a good horse?"

"Yes."

"He's a good horse, but he's not the best horse for you. Quin is an amazing horse, but ever since I got him — ever since I wasn't too much older than you — I've liked different horses. I've always loved grooming Quin, and working on the ground with him, but he's not my favourite kind of horse to ride."

"*Really?* Not like riding *Quin?*"

I shrug. "It's just me, kid. It's probably messed up, but horses like Banks have always been more my speed."

Her eyes open wide. "So, I could ride Quin, and you could ride Banks, and we'd each be on our favourite kind of horse."

"If you're cool with it."

"I'm very, completely, absolutely cool with it."

I smile. "It's a deal then. But ..."

"But what?"

"But, I've been grooming Quin every day since I got here and he's very clean, so it's still on you to groom Banks for me before our ride."

As I leave the stall, she's redoubling her efforts with the curry comb and humming a little tune.

***

The ride is a hit.

I see a whole new side of all the kids. Patrick is all giggles. "This is so slippery!" he yells from Milford's back and promptly slides off the wrong side of the pony.

As soon as Patrick's weight leaves him, the good-natured pony stops in his tracks, turns his head back to check out his young rider, then waits while Patrick scrambles back up.

Once we've established that Patrick can, indeed, just clamber back onto Milford, the rest of us continue our ride while he slides off and hauls himself back on as often as he likes.

And I do mean the rest of us.

When we all gathered next to the huge tree stump the kids use as a mounting block, Ali got in line behind Violet and in front of Patrick.

"Get out of my way!" Patrick hadn't yet figured out he could mount just by jumping.

"No. I got here first. It's my turn."

Violet sighed. "But you don't ride, Ali."

"I do today."

"You never ride for Martha."

"Martha never let us ride bareback."

And that was it. Ali was on.

She and Cressy are a vision — the pretty grey pony picking her way daintily through the long grass as well behaved as if Ali rode her every single day of the year, and Ali's long skirt lying on the pony's back, rippling in the breeze.

Violet rides on the other side of me, and even though it's the first time I've seen her ride without a saddle, it's also the most relaxed I've ever seen her.

When I watched her on Banks, her back was straight as could be. Her arms were set in place. Her heels were jammed down. Technically everything was in the right spot, but nothing moved.

Now she turns to talk to me and automatically adjusts her grip on the reins and the angle of her elbows to keep following Quin's mouth. Her back could be straighter, and her heels aren't down, but her hips follow the horse and he's walking in a forward, easy gait with his head held at a natural angle.

They're both happy. Which is all I want.

I'm liking Banks more all the time. His walk is peppy. He throws in the occasional jig, which I know I shouldn't encourage, and which Violet wouldn't enjoy, but I love his eagerness and energy level.

As we cross the open part of the field, I keep him to a walk so we can stay together as a group, but as we approach the line of trees, I relax my hips and hands and let him trot forward.

"Auntie Hazel!" Violet's voice is anxious, Ali's is surprised, Patrick's has a "wait-for-me" tone to it.

"Follow me!" I call. I'm not worried about them. The most any of their horses will do is move into a more energetic walk. It's such a relief to know they're all on reliable mounts — particularly to know that nervous Violet is on the world's best babysitter.

Banks breaks through the line of trees to the stream that meanders behind them. I know this stream. I charted its path for geography class in grade four. It's not big enough to have a name — other than "the stream" or "the creek" or "the brook" on all the various farms it runs through. Still, despite how narrow it is, and how, in certain spots, it can dry to a trickle in heat like we're experiencing now, it travels a good long way — starting at the County's famous Lake on the Mountain and skirting settlements, forcing the construction of culverts and bridges on the County roads and, like on our farm, shaping the fields and paddocks more definitely than any fence could do.

It only occurs to me to wonder what Banks thinks of water as we reach the ledge leading down to the stream and he flicks his ears forward and snorts. I close my legs around him and prepare to kick, to grunt, to growl, but none of that's necessary. He lowers his nose and rushes down the incline and I swear he sighs as the cool water swirls around his legs.

Quin appears next, and I knew he wouldn't be a problem, because this is one ride I did frequently with him all those years ago. Sure enough he charges in beside Banks, and Cressy follows him with her nose tight against his hind end.

Milford's the one who gives us trouble. Maybe we've found the limit to this pony's perfection? He dithers and paws at the top. He backs up a step, then moves forward, then back again.

Patrick goes red in the face with the effort of squeezing his sides.

Finally Milford lets out a ringing whinny as though to say, "I want it on the record that I don't like this," then I swear he closes his eyes and slides in. Once in, he's all bravado — pawing at the water and splashing everybody else.

I lead them in a single-file train along the stream. Right before the spot where I'm going to take them back up the bank to head home, the trees grow close up to the water and it widens and deepens. Quin knows the drill. He stretches out his neck and swims the short distance to where he can stand again. Violet gasps.

"Just hold his mane!" I tell her.

She floats along with the big horse and they both emerge on the far side streaming water. "Come on!" she calls to her siblings. "It's so fun, and I'm nice and cool now."

One by one we cross, with me last. Banks' dark coat makes him look like a seal when he carries me back up out of the water, through the strip of trees and into the farthest part of the open field.

The three kids ride ahead of me. I watch their straight backs and their little legs dangling along their horses' barrels. I watch the sun hit the animals' rumps and think how soft their coats will feel after this. I listen to the rhythm of the chatter going back and forth between Violet, and Patrick, and Ali.

I don't want to leave.

Picture it covered in snow, I tell myself.

Beautiful. I bet Cressy drives. She could pull a sleigh.

I'd need to quit my job in Vancouver. Sell my condo.

I'll work for Trent. I'm used to living in the trailer. I can stay there until Thanksgiving, at least ... if Aggie will let me.

Good point. Aggie. She, and Brody, and the kids, have their own lives. They're on vacation right now, but they have to go back to real life. I'll still be alone.

But I'll be alone at *home.*

I find I don't have an easy comeback for this one.

Why not enjoy what you have right now?

Milford grabs a mouthful of grass so long the ends hit Cressy, and both Patrick and Ali shake with giggles.

I lay my hand on Banks' warm neck and let my nieces and nephew lead us home.

Fourteen

AGGIE'S WAITING AT THE BARN.

This has got to be a moment a mother dreams of — right? Your children, in the outdoors, getting fresh air and exercise, learning independence within safe boundaries, laughing with each other instead of bickering.

Aggie should be pulling out her phone, taking surreptitious video.

Thanking me.

When I ride up on Banks — prepared to accept her gratitude — she narrows her eyes and asks, "What have you done?"

What have I done? Where does she want me to start?

- Convinced Ali to actually ride her pony — that's one.

- Found the right horse to give Violet confidence and make her enjoy riding — that's another.

- Discovered how Banks likes to be ridden so he's happy and controllable — that's worth something.

"*This* came while you were out." Aggie's a smart woman. She knows holding up a phone screen, in the glaring sun, while I'm on the back of a horse several feet away will not allow me to actually read or comprehend the contents of said screen.

Rather than tell her so, I just lift my eyebrows in a silent, *Really?*

"You. Are. So. F ..." The kids are all sitting on their mounts watching us. "... *Fru*strating," she finishes.

It's all I can do not to laugh out loud as Aggie has to deal with her own, no-cursing rules. But I know laughing would just make her more *frustrated*, so I refrain.

"Kids!" I call. "Who had fun?"

"Whoo-hoo!" they all yell. "All of us!" Ali adds.

"Great! Since you did such a good grooming job before we rode, and since the horses have gotten nice and clean in the stream, all you have to do now is turn them out."

Another "whoo-hoo!" goes up.

"However, you need to take care of Banks as well as your three, since your mom and I are going for a swim."

"You are?" Violet asks.

"We are?" Aggie says.

"Your mom didn't get to cool down in the stream like we did, and I think she's a bit *hot* — amirite, Aggie?"

She gives me a tight smile. "You could say that."

"So," I slide off Banks' gleaming back. "Who am I giving these reins to?"

"Oh, me! Me! Me!" Violet darts forward. It seems she's happy to take ownership of the horse as long as she doesn't have to ride him and I'm fine with that as he has very good stable manners. They all do. Likely thanks to Martha.

I probably owe her an apology.

One more thing to add to my things-to-work-on-to-be-a-better-person list.

Oh well — it's already so long one more thing won't make much of a difference.

***

Aggie's simmering and it's making me hot, too.

She's breathing very deliberately, and deeply ... and loudly. And she's stomping. These hard-packed trails are perfect for near-silent walking in rubber-soled shoes, but nobody's told Aggie that.

She glances back toward the barn once, and waves as one of the kids notices her. I follow her second glance — we can still see them, but just barely.

As soon as we're far enough around the bend that the trees block our view of the kids — and vice versa — she turns to me. "I am so angry with you."

Here's the thing. I'm not nice. I know that. But that's the point — I know it. I admit it. I don't try to hide it. I own it.

In this particular moment, I can honestly say I don't think I've done anything at all to earn my sister-in-law's anger.

Part of me wants to ask her why, and part of me wants to just walk away.

She makes the decision for me, by again holding up her phone and saying, "Look!" except this time, at least, she hands it to me, and we're in the shade, so I can actually read it.

I recognize it — it's the contract from Trent. Because I know what to scan for, it takes me less than a minute to extract the critical information, namely when they want to take over the property and how much they're paying. Everything else is boilerplate, written in unnecessarily complicated language. I thought Trent would send me the contract and I'd walk Aggie and Brody through it, but I'm OK with him putting her on the main email.

It seems, for some reason, that she's not.

I hand her phone back. "I've looked. Can you tell me what's bugging you so much?"

"What's bugging me? How can you even ask that?" She starts walking and I follow one step behind. "I mean, it's irrelevant, because Brody owns half of everything, and you can't do this without him signing, and he won't sign, so I don't know why I'm even mad — I should just ignore it, forget it, but I *am* mad ..."

She stops and looks at me. "I was so stupid. I thought you'd help — solve all our problems — I should never have trusted you."

"Sorry, what?"

"Trusted you. I knew I shouldn't."

"Is this trust? Is this how you trust Brody? If so, my poor brother."

"Don't deflect."

"Don't accuse."

"It's not an accusation — it's a fact. You're trying — no, you *agreed* — to sell part of our farm off to some total stranger."

I have a sudden flashback to a Model UN conference where Aggie was representing Alvonia. She didn't read, or read too quickly, or ... I don't really know what ... a clause saying the EU would give her country money to explore waste disposal options. Aggie read it as the EU saying they would dispose of their waste in her country. She delivered an impassioned speech calling out the poor kid assigned to be the head of the European Commission.

He cried.

I'm getting a tiny taste of how that kid felt. "I, what?"

"Listen, Hazel, I know it's a lot of money, and I know we need money, but ... how would this even work? How can they have the sugar shack which is right in the middle of our farm — our home? What were you thinking?"

"Two words, Aggie."

"What?"

"Model UN."

"That makes no sense, and that's not even two words. It's a word and an acronym."

"OK, I'll add a third. Alvonia."

"Alvonia? What? ... wait ... really?" She peers at her screen.

"You said it yourself, Ags. It would never work. Even if I wanted to, I couldn't just sell off a patch in the middle of the farm. What you're looking at is a contract for a six-month rental. It starts now, so they can get summer shots. They have it all fall, to get autumn footage, and they have it into the winter so they can film snow."

"That money is for six months?"

I nod.

"But it's so much."

"Not to them." I point at the phone. "If you read right to the bottom —" I pause to let it sink in that she didn't even read the top properly, "— you'll see they have an option to renew. If so, that will be more money."

"I ..." She starts, but fails to finish, so I pick up. "We've known each other a long time, Ags. Over the years you've seen the worst of me — and there's a lot of that to see — but on this particular issue, all I've tried to do is help the farm. Which, hopefully, means helping you and Brody, and the kids." I sigh. "I wish you didn't dislike me so much that even this becomes contentious."

I shake my head. "Whatever. It's been a long day, and I'm hot and sweaty, and the entire Gimme Shelter volunteer committee will be arriving in less than two hours, so I'm jumping in the pond."

To emphasize my statement, I stride along to the offshoot of the path leading to the pond, peeling my t-shirt off over my head as I go.

**

There's nothing like the weightlessness of being fully immersed in water. After a long run, or a long ride, or a long day, I can close my eyes and imagine the soreness leaching out of the soles of my feet, the stiffness swirling out of my neck and shoulders.

Not to mention the grime and the sweat of the day ... gone.

If only I could say the same of my troubles.

I open one eye.

Aggie's swimming toward me.

I exhale, flex my feet, roll my shoulders — *you're floating, you're light as a feather, you're carefree, you're Zen.*

"Are you skinny-dipping?"

"If I was, would you stay away?"

"Hazel! You can't just skinny-dip in broad daylight when Brody or the kids could show up ..."

"Aggie, chill. I'm wearing my bra and underwear." I don't tell her they're white, and now wet, so essentially might as well not be there at all.

She swims closer and I notice she's holding a cheap inflatable ball under each arm. "Here —" she bats one to me and pushes the other under the water. In a second she's upright, seemingly suspended in the water. When I lift my eyebrows, she says, "Sit on it."

My struggle to push the ball down is undignified, and I suspect Aggie sees a lot of white skin and see-through underwear in the process, but for once she stays quiet, and when I've finally found my balance on the ball, the calm, gentle bobbing is well worth it.

"Nice, right?" Aggie asks.

"Much better than the yoga ball I have for an office chair at work."

Work. If Aggie was a Jack Russell terrier her ears would have perked at the word. I probably shouldn't have even introduced the topic. "You want to talk about that?" Aggie asks. "Work?"

"No." I lift my voice at the end of the word.

Aggie nods. "I thought so. What's going on?"

"I left." She nods. She knows that part.

"I lied." She lifts her eyebrows.

"I told them my appendix burst."

"Why?"

"I think it's usually because of an infection."

"Hazel!"

I sigh. "It wasn't just because of Tom — because of the engagement — that I left. It was because of my friends, and my life." I shake my head. "Except that's not really true. It was because of me. I was running away from myself. Which, of course, also meant leaving work behind."

I wait for Aggie's judgment. For her to point out the obvious truth that if one isn't happy with oneself, ditching one's fiancé and work doesn't make one a better person.

"I don't hate you," she says.

"Oh," I say. "Thanks?"

"Well, you said you wish I didn't hate you so much that I'd make the film crew thing contentious. For the record, I don't hate you."

"I think I said 'dislike.'"

"Yes. Well. Either way. Full disclosure — I have, sometimes, disliked you. Which, of course, was wrong, even though at the time I told myself it wasn't. Lately I've been finding I sometimes like you, so I feel some guilt about disliking you before."

I must be getting soft, because Aggie's qualified admission that she kind of likes me these days sets up a little ache behind my breastbone. I blink, and pretend it's the bright sun making me do it. "Don't bother feeling guilty. I wasn't very nice."

"Yeah. About that."

"About what?"

"What's with all the 'I'm not nice,' stuff? You've been going on about it quite a bit."

"What? You're surprised I'm admitting it?" Before she can answer, I continue. "It's true. I was blind to it myself. This ... thing ... happened back in Vancouver, and I suddenly saw everything perfectly clearly. How I'd surrounded myself with really not-very-nice people. How mean they were, and how I was just like them. What a terrible person Tom was, and how I was willing to marry him. And my job — well it's not as though I do meaningful work like raising children, or teaching them, or growing food."

She's giving me a skeptical squint, as I push on. "And I was getting these nostalgic flashes. About this place — the County, and the farm — and about Brody and the kids ..."

She opens her mouth, and I laugh, "... and you, too. So I left town. Didn't face anyone, or tie up any loose ends. Just bolted. Which I guess makes me irresponsible as well as unkind."

"What a load of crap!" Both Aggie's words and her vehemence surprise me so much I tip back off my ball. It shoots straight up in the air, thwacking my chin on the way, and I have to scramble to retrieve it.

When I've wrestled it back into place, and am panting with the exertion, I ask, "What part of it is a load of crap?"

"This whole, 'boo-hoo, I'm not nice,' thing." She holds up her fingers and begins listing off: "You're stubborn. You're tough. You're blunt ..." As much as I admire her ability to balance with both hands out of the water, I'm not sure how high I want her to count.

"Sorry, I thought you were saying you *didn't* dislike me."

"Right, that's the point. Those aren't negative things — not necessarily. It's all how you interpret them. Or ... how you're taught to interpret them."

"What do you mean?"

"Who told you you're not nice?"

"Nobody — that's the point — none of the people I was spending time with are nice either. I just figured it out for myself."

"Really? Is that true? Nobody ever told you that?"

Somewhere deep in the part of my brain that keeps feeding me sensations of nostalgia, are sayings from my childhood:

- "You're not going to get ahead by being nice," — that was as I waited to ride into the ring to play musical poles at my first-ever horse show.

- "People might not like you, but that's OK because they'll respect you," — that was the night before my first Model UN conference.

- "You're a lot like me, which is good, because nobody will ever push you around," — that was too often to remember.

Aggie nods. "Your mother, right? The reason I know is that she had Brody convinced of the opposite — that he was weak. That everyone would walk all over him. That he couldn't run the farm by himself and might as well sell it."

"But ..." I shake my head. "I mean, he's not. He's great. He's so strong — and not just physically, doing all that hard labour — but being a farmer is tough. Dealing with the weather, and animals, and people, and he's also a father ..."

"Right," Aggie says.

"What do you mean, 'right?'"

"I mean, that's how you see him. What if he — what if other people — don't see you the way you see yourself?"

I narrow my eyes. "You think bad things about me. The whole time I've been here I've been getting little comments back from the kids, and from Brody, and Gus, about how I'll react to things — what I'll say or do."

She shrugs. "What can I say? That's my weakness. I'm overly controlling. I'm trying to get better, but I still do it.

It's hard for me not to worry about things, then to judge, then to say things I shouldn't."

Her admission throws me off guard. "You're not that bad ..." I say.

"It seems to me that a nasty person wouldn't try to comfort me." She laughs. "Really, Hazel, it's nice of you but you don't have to try to make me feel better. We have a therapist to help us work through Ali's transition and I'm learning more about myself than anything else."

I snap my fingers. "Ali. Violet said you weren't sure how I'd react to her."

"Which is an absolute perfect example of how you're actually a much nicer person than me. I can be very defensive about my daughter. And you've honestly been more accepting and supportive than anybody else. Well, except Gus who, of course, is perfect."

"Right," I say. "Gus. You warned me not to break his heart. You obviously think I'm not good enough for him."

"Or, I obviously don't want Gus's heart broken."

"By me."

"By somebody who ten days ago was living and engaged in Vancouver and, if I'm understanding correctly, is still employed there."

When she puts it that way. "Point taken. But ..."

"You're determined not to be a nice person, aren't you?"

"It's not that. It's just that there are all these examples ..."

"Lay them on me."

"Yes. Fine. OK." I shift on my ball and try to hold my balance so I can list them off on my fingers like Aggie did. It's immediately evident that's going to lead to a repeat of the ball cannoning out from under me, so I give up. I hold out my fingers under water instead. "I used to love beating people at Model UN. *Love* it. I took active pleasure from humiliating them."

"That," Aggie says. "Was Model UN. They would all love to have beaten you. You were just better than them."

"You had to tell me not to swear around your kids. Who swears around kids?"

"Um, just about everybody!" She laughs. "Nothing is sacred anymore. We took them to the homecoming game at the university and the guy in front of us kept dropping f-bombs then turning around and saying, 'Sorry! I keep forgetting there are kids here — shit!'"

I laugh, too, but persist. "When you told me to stop, instead of feeling guilty, I was annoyed, and pissed off, and I still sometimes really, really, want to swear in front of them."

"Welcome to the club. You're human. You may even be qualified to be a parent one day."

"OK, those weren't great examples. But this next one ..." I bite my lip. I shake my head. I've been glossing over it so long it's hard to bring it up.

"You made out with Robert Decker back in eighth grade when I had a crush on him."

"What? No! *Robert Decker?* Are you serious? He was the worst ..."

She holds up her hand. "Whoa, whoa! Don't say anything! I want to preserve my rose-tinted memories of Robert." She continues. "If it wasn't making out with Robert, maybe you were the one who used to break into Jenny Chen's locker and steal her White-Out."

"That was a thing?"

Aggie sighs. "Fine! You killed somebody and buried the body behind the sugar shack."

"Aggie!"

"Hazel!" She shakes her head. "I'm starting to think you're quite a goody two-shoes ... it's kind of embarrassing."

"I abandoned Quin."

"Quin?"

"Yes, Quin. My horse. Well, he was supposed to be my horse, but I ..." I lift both hands, then, after a near-capsize from my ball, slap them back down quickly.

"Last I checked, downtown Vancouver isn't the best place for a horse. Plus, you know I do accept your eTransfers every month to pay for his keep." Aggie says.

"It's not that, Aggie. It wasn't just when I left. It was from Day One. My dad brought me home this amazing horse. The best horse there is, really. And I just ... didn't ride him. Didn't show him. Left the farm every day to ride other horses. And, then — yeah — took off to Vancouver and left him here."

"Oh Hazel."

That familiar old reaction rises in me — an Aggie-inspired mix of frustration, and irritation, and anger. "You're being smug." I add. "Which wasn't very nice of me to say."

She lifts her eyebrows. "I don't know about not being nice — you're telling the truth. Although I wouldn't call it smug. More like incredulous that somebody who's supposed to be smart — who, specifically, is supposed to be *horse* smart — could be so dense."

"What do you mean?"

"Quin is happy. This is where he belongs, and this is the life he likes. Low-key, quiet, easy, relaxed. Quin wouldn't have liked being shipped across the country, and he wasn't born to show. It might sound harsh, but it's true to say Quin was always too boring for the way you liked to ride ... but he was just right for me, and you let me ride him."

I open my mouth but she rushes ahead. "And now you let my daughter ride him, which I can see makes her so happy."

I don't particularly like being called dense. I mutter, "Yeah, well that's because somebody bought her completely the wrong horse."

"Yup." Aggie nods. "Me. Being controlling again. I thought she needed a horse who would challenge her. I thought she needed to be strong."

"Violet has diamonds in her core."

"I know." Aggie blinks. "I couldn't see it, but you could. You just motored in here from Vancouver and you *got* my whole family in a way that I couldn't see them."

"*Hmm* ... I wouldn't say I have a handle on Patrick."

She laughs. "You had him at the Lucky Charms."

I wrinkle my nose. "I have to admit that was a genius move — that's why they pay me the big bucks."

"About that ..." Aggie says. "What's up?"

"What's up is I'm supposed to be at my desk the day after tomorrow, and it's a five-day drive."

"Ri-i-i-ght ..." she says. "So are you quitting? Or am I driving you to the airport tomorrow and keeping your adorable little car as payment for my services?"

"I ..." Butterflies bat around my gut. I start again. "I'd like ..." God this is stupid. If I was talking to someone else having this much trouble getting their words out, I'd tell them to ...

"Spit it out!" Aggie snaps her fingers.

"I'd like to stay." I force myself to meet her eyes. "If I can. I mean, if you'd let me crash in the trailer for a while longer."

Aggie smiles. "If you hadn't asked, I would have insisted."

"Right." My tone is sarcastic, but I'm smiling, too.

Aggie shrugs. "I have no idea how to manage a film crew, the kids would miss you, and there's that whole Gus thing."

I snort. "Gus. Indeed."

"Wait a minute ... less than 24 hours ago Gus turned your shirt inside-out. Please don't tell me you're already tired of him, because if so ..."

"Not me him," I say. "He me."

"Sorry, are we in a Dr. Seuss book?"

I exhale so forcefully it rattles my lips. "What I'm trying to say is that I spent today driving around festival sites, hoping to come across Gus, and far from bumping into him, I'm pretty sure he was actively avoiding me." I sigh. "It would seem Gus may have turned more than my t-shirt inside-out, and if anyone's heart is going to be broken it could be mine."

"Your hard, shriveled little heart?" Aggie reaches for my arm. "Sorry! I couldn't resist. That is seriously the best news ever!"

"It's the best news that Gus is avoiding me and breaking my heart?"

"You're not as mean as you think you are, Haze, but you're also not as smart."

"By which you mean?"

"By which I mean I sometimes know things you don't."

"Aggie ..."

"Gus was at the board offices in the city today, taking a 'Teaching LGBTQ Students' workshop, so he wasn't even in the County to be avoiding you and, also, right before I came out to the barn he texted to ask if there was anything he could bring to the meeting tonight, so that definitely doesn't sound like he's avoiding you."

My chest is doing this weird, achy thing. "He was taking a Teaching LGBTQ Students workshop?"

Aggie nods.

My voice is doing a strange thing as well. It seems I can only whisper. "*He. Is. So. Nice.*"

Aggie nods.

Then, in a zero-to-sixty move, my heart zooms into rapid thump mode. "He's coming to the meeting tonight."

"Yes."

"Oh my god, I'm ..."

"Not your best self." Aggie reaches out and gives me a good hard shove that topples me from my ball. "I call the right to be controlling on this one — go!"

I'm splashing in the water, mind racing, and for the first time I have some sympathy for my clients who come to me in a chaotic state, unable to figure out what to do next.

"I need to call work," I gasp. "I need to get pizza ..."

"You need to get clean, and get dry, and put on half-decent clothes." Aggie's already swimming back toward the deck, and I'm automatically following her.

"But ..."

"Agreed," she says. "You need to call work. You can do that later. They're three hours behind anyway. And Brody will get the pizza."

I haul myself out onto the warm wood, splashing what feels like half the pond with me. "He will?"

Aggie's eyes flit from my feet up my body, locking onto my face. "Hazel ..."

I forgot the wet, white undergarments. "Sorry!" I cross my arms over my chest. "I can't put those filthy clothes back on. I'll sprint back to the trailer."

"Please do," Aggie says.

I start running then stop, call back. "I'll pay Brody back for the pizza."

"Yes! Go!"

I run until my bare feet hit the dirt of the path, then stop again. "And Aggie, for the love of god, tell Brody it can't be Jo-jo's!"

"Now who's being controlling!" I laugh as her words float after me but I don't stop — I don't have time.

Fifteen

IT'S STILL ROASTING, sweltering, steam-bath hot by the time everyone convenes on the front porch, but thanks to Aggie at least I got a cool, clean start and am wearing fresh clothes — in reality they're already wilting, but they were fresh a few minutes ago.

The bottom of my feet, the backs of my knees, and the insides of my elbows are clammy with humidity, and it's not even worth discussing my armpits.

Still, everyone's in the same boat, I tell myself.

And, really, the heat is giving my skin a lovely sheen — a healthy glow.

"Auntie Hazel, you look really sweaty!" Patrick peers up at me from under the tangled mop that is his bangs.

"Didn't I just hear your mom wanting you to have a bath?"

"No-o-o ...!" He jumps back, but I've already got my hand on his shoulder. "Yoo-hoo! Aggie! I found Patrick!"

He scowls up at me. "Thanks a lot."

I shrug. "You scratch my back, I'll scratch yours."

"What does that even mean?"

Before I can answer, Aggie appears and takes her son by his other shoulder. "Thanks, Hazel."

As I watch him trudge away, I don't feel mean at all. Aggie's given me a whole new outlook on my actions. I was just helping my nephew understand natural consequences. In the long run, I was actually doing him a favour.

Not only have I been nice to Patrick — I'm here to do a really, significantly nice thing. A win-win-win thing. Something that helps Flora and Peace, who are swaying gently on the porch swing, and Brenda and Kumar, sunk deeply into Muskoka chairs, and the community at large, and even Trent's company ... and it would help Gus, too, if he was here.

Which he's not.

But that's fine. I can handle it. I know he knows the meeting's on, and I know he knows what time it starts, and we can't wait all day for lollygaggers ... even if they are lollygagging on their way home from an LGBTQ workshop ... and, yes, I still go a little weak in the knees thinking of Gus's beautiful face, and strong body, spending the day in a classroom learning how he can be an even better teacher to kids who really need him.

"Speech!" That's the problem with having a high-powered group of volunteers — they don't do Muskoka-chair-sitting or porch-swing-swaying for long. "Speech! Speech!" Peace started but now they're all joining in.

I hold up my hands, call, "Fine! OK! You win!" Violet helped me rig a sheet at the far end of the porch and I project the promotional trailer from Trent's company's charitable project from last year, showing the adorable owlets and the enthusiastic researcher.

It doesn't take long for the penny to drop. Like I say, they're a high-powered, motivated group.

"Are you telling us you secured this sponsorship for the festival this year?" Flora asks.

"Yes," I say.

"How much is it?"

Brenda, who's still watching the video, yells, "Twenty-five thousand dollars!" She turns to Flora. "Maybe watch the video?"

I nod. "Twenty-five thousand."

"But that's ..." Kumar falters. "That's more than we can even spend this year."

"Yes, well, I've put together a sort of proposal-slash-report for my friend's company showing how we would use the funds. Having gone through the books —" I wrinkle my nose at the thought of all those loose papers and almost-illegible scribbles, "— I have to tell you there are some outstanding debts to pay off. Then there are this year's expenses. Kumar's quite right that still doesn't add up to twenty-five-thousand dollars, so I have some suggestions of investments we can make now, that will help with future festivals. I wanted to discuss that over pizza — which we can afford now, by the way — if the pizza ever arrives ..."

I take a step back and several hard edges dig into my back. I turn around to face a stack of pizza boxes ... held by Gus.

"Oh!" There was a breeze here earlier, but I don't know where it's gone. "Gus." I put a hand to my cheek. It feels sticky. *Glow*, I tell myself. *It's not sweat, it's radiance.* "You got us pizza. Thank you."

"You got us twenty-five thousand dollars?"

"I, um, yes ..."

"And not just that!" Aggie's on the porch carrying a box bigger than the pizza boxes all stacked together. "This arrived just a few minutes before you all got here!"

She sets the box on the edge of the porch and starts pulling out t-shirts. They have the Gimme Shelter logo splashed across the front, and they say "VOLUNTEER" in huge letters on the back. Trent's company's logo is small, tucked under the "R" of "volunteer."

A throng forms around the pizza boxes on the table and the box of t-shirts beside them. My volunteer team mainly wants the shirts, while my nieces and my nephew

— wet hair leaving drips all over his shoulders — are rooting around for their favourite flavour of pizza.

"... same-day t-shirt printing?" Peace is asking.

Kumar's nodding. "Along with same-day delivery, I'm thinking."

"Wow!" For once the capable, down-to-earth, unflappable Brenda looks excited. "This is really happening!"

"Yes. It is." I don't look at her, though. I lock eyes with Gus and I savour the feeling as my stomach does a long, slow, flip-flop.

**

Brenda plugs her laptop into the projector. It's amazing how quick and easy it is to spend money — it doesn't take long for the group to come to an agreement about the use of the newfound riches.

Pizza mostly eaten, festival t-shirts claimed, but not worn, since the heat makes any additional layers unbearable, the assembled group breaks into clusters.

Kumar and Brenda. Peace and Flora. Aggie, Brody, and Gus. The kids weave in and out, around legs and furniture, up and down between the porch and the lawn.

I listen to the low hum of conversation, with the sing-song of crickets as a backdrop. I watch these people I've come to like so much, with their eyes lit up and even if their hair sticks to their warm faces, they're beautiful — glowing — to me. One, in particular.

"Hazel?"

I blink and realize the beautiful one has asked me a question.

"Yes?"

He indicates a bare board next to my perch on the edge of the porch. "Can I sit here?"

"Oh! Of course." I'm aware of Aggie and Brody rounding up children, trying to herd them through the front door. It must be time to brush teeth.

I clear my throat. "So, Aggie told me you were at a workshop in the city today. How was it?"

He nods. "Really good. A lot of the material was common sense, but meeting other teachers and picking their brains — hearing their experiences — was great. I want to run a GSA this year, and another participant had started one at her school last year, so it was great to talk to her. But ..."

"But, what?"

"The workshop was great, but I'd always rather be here."

The clearing around the farmhouse is in full gloaming. In one spot a final shaft of sunlight makes everything around it bright and golden, however, a glance at the sky shows the brightest of the stars shining through. For a moment, a breeze lifts the hair off my shoulders and reminds me what it is to be cool.

I nod. "There's something about this place."

"Something about certain parts of this place," he adds, and I instantly picture the whitewashed interior of the sugar shack. Remember the coolness of its floorboards. Relive a flash of desire which is still in my eyes when they meet his. I can tell because his gaze mirrors it back to me.

A burst of laughter reminds me we're not alone and I shake my head and take a deep breath. "Well, I was certainly glad to hear you were at the workshop today because I kept seeing grey pickups going the opposite direction from wherever I was heading and I thought it was you avoiding me."

"Absolutely not. In fact, I saw a neon green hatchback in the city today, and I had to talk myself out of following it."

"Really?" It's extraordinarily nice to find that not only were my worries unfounded, but the opposite is true. While I was coming around to liking Gus, he kept liking me the whole time. It's an amazing feeling.

I know I'm blushing and I don't even try to stop it — don't even try to hide it from him. He's nice and he likes me — I want to enjoy that for a minute or two.

"...tie Hazel?" I'm so love-doped that I'm a couple of beats behind tuning into Violet saying my name. "Auntie Hazel? Are you listening?"

"Yes, of course sweetie. What is it?"

"I answered the phone, and it was for you. It's your boss from Vancouver. He says since he hasn't heard anything he expects he'll see you in the office the day after tomorrow."

Her brow isn't the only furrowed one. Lines also knit Gus's forehead. Violet shakes her head. "That didn't sound right, so I told him I'd get you to talk to him."

For the second time this evening I have less breath than I need to speak. "Oh. Thanks for finding me ..."

"It's not right, is it Auntie Hazel?"

"No. I mean, it's a misunderstanding. It's something I have to clear up." Gus is full-on frowning now.

"You'd better talk to him right away," Violet says. "Because to get back to work on Monday means you'd have to leave tomorrow!"

I turn to Gus. "Yes, Hazel, it sounds like you'd better talk to him right away."

"I will." I look back and forth between the two of them. "I'll just be gone a minute. Two at the most. Don't go anywhere. I'll be right back ..." This over my shoulder as I head for the house, and the kitchen phone, acutely aware my face is burning for a very different reason than just a few seconds ago. Back when I was dreamily happy. Back when I was busy mutually falling in love ... or at least very strong reciprocal affection. *Very* strong.

Maybe this is for the best, I tell myself. At least now everything will be out in the open. At least I can be honest with Devon and commit to my new life here.

Right. This will be good. I roll my shoulders back, pull the screen door open and step into the kitchen to find the phone resting on the counter where Violet left it.

***

"Hey," I say. "Devon."

"No," he says.

"No, what?"

"No more beating around the bush. No more evasion. Just tell me — are you not coming back?" Before I can say anything, he continues. "I'm not trying to be a jerk here, Haze. I just need to know. You know — so I can run my business. So I can get my clients taken care of."

Just like that, I see Devon in a different light. I see my job in a different light. I even see my clients in a different light — *some* of them, anyway.

Aggie's positive spin on my own behaviour is having the knock-on effect of me giving other people in my life the benefit of the doubt.

Devon isn't mean, or bad. He's demanding, has high expectations, and is sometimes too honest. But he's that way to do the best work for his clients, and to build the best reputation for his business and, I guess, to keep me gainfully employed.

I feel a stab of shame. "You're right, Devon. I'm sorry."

"Excuse me, is this actually Hazel Edwards I'm speaking to? I didn't know 'sorry' was in your vocabulary."

"I *am* sorry. I guess I've been a bit like some of our clients. Trying to figure my life out and not doing it the best way."

He laughs. "Sure, OK. Some of our clients are like that. The rest are just narcissistic, entitled, self-important egomaniacs." He pauses. "However, what I really need to know is whether your figured-out life includes working for me."

I take a deep breath. "It doesn't involve living in Vancouver." Then, the first time I've said it positively, definitely: "I'm moving back home."

"Right." He sighs and I can picture the quick double-rub of his temples, the way he manually smooths his brow. "I wish you had just come out and told me. It would have been much easier."

I was bracing for anger. I was bracing for sarcasm. Or lecture on lack of professionalism. What I wasn't anticipating was this calm resignation.

"Will you keep working for me remotely, or do you want to move on completely?"

"Excuse me?"

"As you know we have fairly regular inquiries from Toronto-based clients. We've helped a select few in the past, but it's not ideal. If you're willing and able to go to Toronto now and then for in-person meetings, you could help us test the waters on opening an Ontario branch."

"Really?" It's true that the first thing I think about is the money. I'm going to need it. However, I also really do like problem-solving. I like helping clients out of the pickles they get themselves into ... at least I like helping *some* of them.

"... can't promise full time," Devon's saying. "At least not at the beginning."

"That's fine!" I think of Trent's offer of work. I think if this is going to be my home, I need to do a lot more helping out around the farm. I think I've just guaranteed the festival will be running next year. "Part-time is perfect for me."

"I got a call from a potential Ontario client today. She was referred by her sister, who lives in Vancouver. I'll make the introduction by email and you can open a file for her, if that works."

"That works."

"Well, I'm glad it works," Devon says, "But why was it so hard to get here? After all these years why couldn't you just talk to me?"

The conversation with Aggie was a game-changer, and it's one I'm still processing. I don't know how to explain all of that to Devon. Then it occurs to me I don't have to. It's not really the past that's important.

"I will from now on." I say it with a promise in my voice.

"OK." I can picture his distinctive nod — a quick chin dip with closed eyes. A surge of fondness wells up in me. I like Devon with all his prickles, so I guess it's possible for other people to like me, with mine. I'm so lucky that one of those people appears to be Gus.

"OK," I answer. There's a bubble of excitement building in me. This is going to be great. I can't wait to tell Aggie and Brody. I can't wait to see the kids' reactions. But I left the person I really want to tell standing outside and I can't wait to get back to him. To give him all the details. To explain everything.

I've got to go.

"I've got to go, Devon, but thanks a bunch. Bye!"

**

Gus isn't where I left him.

Neither is Violet.

I count everybody on the porch. Kumar, Peace, Flora, Brenda, Aggie — with Ali lifted to her hip in a flashback to toddler days, Brody — holding Patrick's hand while my nephew's free hand reaches for a box of cookies Flora brought.

"Have you seen Gus?" I ask Aggie.

"Yes, of course. You were talking to him."

I bite my lip — *don't yell at her.* "After that. Recently."

She looks around. "No-o-o ..." Then seems to pick up on my bit lip, my foot tapping the porch boards. "What happened?"

"Work called. Violet answered. She came to tell me they were expecting me back Monday."

Aggie's eyes widen. "In front of Gus?"

I nod. "I talked to Devon, then I came back and Gus is gone."

"You talked to your boss?"

"Oh for god's sake, Aggie!" I squint my eyes closed, shake my head. "Sorry, sorry, sorry. I'm stressed. The work conversation was good, and I'll tell you later, but I have a bad feeling ... Gus had this look on his face ... and it was all going so well until then ..."

She reaches her free hand out and takes mine. "It'll be OK, Hazel. How far can he get without his truck?"

His truck.

Aggie squeezes my hand. "Go check if it's still here." She jerks her chin toward Ali, draped over her side. "This one is out like a light. I need to drop her in bed, but after that I'll help if you haven't found him."

***

Gus's pickup is nowhere to be found.

Instead of being hidden behind Brody and Aggie's big crew cab pickup, like I hoped it was, there's just a rectangle of empty gravel big enough to contain a regular pick up, and next to it Kumar's reliable old Corolla which he used to carpool all the other volunteers here.

Oh, no.

I walk back to the house and find Aggie rearranging dishes in the dishwasher. She takes one look at my face and says, "Go up to Violet's room. She wasn't asleep when I came down. Maybe he told her where he was going."

I take the steps two at a time, walk by the bathroom where my brother is standing beside Patrick at the sink. "No, keep brushing — that was only twenty seconds ..."

Past Ali's room where a quick glance shows her starfished across her bed, hair fanned across her pillow.

I force my steps to slow before Violet's room. I stop in her doorway.

"Auntie Hazel?"

"Hey, sweetie." My feet land on first a damp towel, then a soaking bathing suit, and finally a soft shag area rug before I reach her bedside.

"You're still here." She's balanced on the fine edge between asleep and awake. Eyes blinking, voice thick and slow.

"Yes, sweetie. I'm staying here."

This elicits a few quick blinks, eyes briefly widening. "For good?"

For good. That's a big question. What if the farm needs to be sold? What if I really am a not-that-great fickle person and I get tired of this place? What if Gus will never speak to me again, and I can't bear living here? That's not what she's asking, though.

"Yes, honey, for good."

Her face relaxes, eyes close. "Oh, good. 'Cause Gus and me were worried."

"Violet, baby. About Gus — do you know where he went?"

She's gone, rolled over. Unlike her sister with limbs flung wide across her bed, Violet curls in, finds security in a nest of her own creation.

I scoop up the bathing suit and towel in my way out.

I might lose the love of my life tonight, but at least I can save my sister-in-law's hardwood floors.

Sixteen

IT'S COMPLETELY ILLOGICAL, but I still go to all the places I associate with Gus on the farm.

First to the pond, where there isn't even a breeze to ruffle the smooth surface.

You're hot — jump in, says an inner voice.

This isn't about you — it's about Gus, says the other.

I'm not convinced it makes a difference, but the superstitious part of me decides I shouldn't do anything for myself until I find Gus.

On impulse I snap a photo of the abandoned dock and quiet pond, then I head to the sugar shack.

***

Talk about bittersweet.

My dad's frequent presence at the shack, vs. the years since he died.

The rise and fall of the building itself — from new-built and promising in somebody's eyes, to disrepair, to the resurrection Gus began, and the changes the film crew will make so it works for the story they're telling.

Gus and I coming together, to Gus and I being so far apart.

I snap a selfie in the middle of the big, white, empty room, before striking out again.

**

The volunteers are piling into Kumar's car when I get back.

"Oh, Hazel honey, we wondered where you were!" I stifle a smile at Peace's greeting. I was never "honey" before I secured the money. Whatever. Don't look a gift horse.

They all step away from the car and surround me. "Great work," "So exciting," "Do so much with the funding," "Can't wait for the festival." Then someone asks, "Where's Gus?"

Fortunately they all answer each other, "Probably dropping something off at community hall," "Double-checking structure at the fairgrounds," "Didn't he say he was going to pick up some of the gym equipment from the school for the kiddie corner?"

Kumar drives off, taking the happy buzz with him, and I'm left feeling an emptiness I haven't experienced since the last time I was back here — when my dad had just died, long after I'd divorced myself from the day-to-day running of the farm, and when all I wanted to do was get back to Vancouver so I could work so much I didn't have to think, and spend my time off work with people so focused on the getting the best meal, the best manicure, the best martini, and the best weekend mountain adventure, that we never had to talk about feelings.

Right now, I'm left with my feelings.

***

He's not at my trailer, which, duh — I didn't think he'd be, but I had to check.

I snap a picture of my little car in front of the empty trailer, then head into the night.

There's nothing like the blackness of a stifling summer night. There are no streetlights out here anyway, no sign of the moon, and the air's so thick with humidity it feels like a fog. I quickly roll up the windows and blast the AC, but even with the fan on full-tilt I can still hear the pattering of headlight-drunk bugs splatting the front of the car.

Gus, Gus, Gus. I wonder if I'm just out hunting him because it's become a challenge. Just an extension of my compulsive goal-setting.

I round a bend and see a pool of light from the first streetlight, and parked under it is a grey pick up. My heart leaps and thuds, and a fleeting wave of nausea travels through me.

So, no. Not just an empty challenge.

It's not his truck. There are probably about a thousand grey pickups in this county at any given time, and this is just one of those.

I want to find his.

The parking lot at the community hall is vacant, and the hall is locked up tight.

I take a photo of my car in front of the steps, fumble the phone, and my contacts screen pops up. With my most recently added contact front and centre. Gus.

Without thinking I text him the photo. **I'm kinda out here looking for you.**

I slap at a mosquito, wipe at the trickle of sweat heading down the back of my neck. That single, solitary photo is not a good representation of the amount of work I've put into looking for Gus.

I send the others. **Looked here ... and here ... Wished you were here.**

This time the mosquito connects, and I yell, "Ow" and jump back into the car to head for the fairgrounds.

My pulse picks up when I see a grey truck parked there until I see it's rocking. And the windows are steamed up. *Please don't let it be Gus, please don't let it be Gus ...*

I sneak forward from my own parked car, although I'm not sure why I'm bothering — whoever is in that truck has no clue I'm out here.

Ugh. I really don't want to get close enough to see anything that's going on inside, but I also want to make sure it's not Gus's truck.

Which ... how? I can pick one particular chestnut horse out of a field of twenty chestnut horses, but I don't know the make, model, or year of Gus's truck. I don't pay attention to wheels or trim.

Wait ... a bumper sticker. Two bumper stickers. One is a picture of a donkey with a hole through the middle. The other proclaims **Redneck on board**.

Phew! Not Gus.

I lift my phone and take a picture of the truck. I'm grinning as I make sure the bumper stickers are fully visible.

Then the flash goes off.

Shit! In this situation, no polite substitute will do.

The truck stops rocking.

Damn!

I run back to the car, jump in, fumble for my keys, struggle to get the key into the ignition, stall it, and finally get it going.

Don't look at the truck, don't look at the truck ...

I accelerate down the deserted street and, eventually, when I'm convinced nobody is following me, pull into a parking lot where I continue all the way around the side of a big brick building before feeling safe enough to send Gus the latest picture.

My heart nearly stopped for a moment when I thought this was your truck.

As glad as I am the love truck wasn't Gus's, I'm also fairly dismayed by being nearly out of places to look for him, and still not finding him.

I've been to everywhere I've ever seen him, and the only other place the volunteers mentioned was the school.

Which ... come to think of it ... I take a fresh look at the brick wall beside me. Yup — the school.

Not a truck in sight.

I do a slow lap around the building to double-check, but the only vehicle is mine, and the building is as dark as a school should be during the summer holidays.

I turn my headlights on the school sign and take a picture. Right before I send it, I notice a text. It's from Violet, sent a few minutes ago. **Auntie Hazel, I just woke up to get a drink of water and I remembered you were in my room asking where Gus was. Did you try his house? I'm turning my phone off now, because my mom will take it away if she finds out I've been texting you this late, but that's where I'd look.**

It makes me want to laugh, and it makes me want to cry, because of course it would be a great suggestion, *if I knew where he lived.*

Then I think of the absurdity of driving around the county as the night wears on looking for a guy I don't even know well enough to know his address.

But I like him. I sigh. Send the final photo. **I don't know where else to go, so I guess I'll have to go home.**

Maybe Aggie will still be awake when I get back. Maybe she'll tell me where Gus lives.

Then I think of the thing Aggie definitely would tell me. Because, sure the series of photos are a gesture of sorts, but there's another gesture which seems simpler but would be way more effective.

I compose another text to Gus. **I'm sorry. I know I haven't been straightforward. Or clear. I'm sure it came as a shock to hear I was supposed to be back at work the day after tomorrow. It was a misunderstanding. Sort of. I can explain more — if you'll give me a chance — but the main thing is I'm not going back Monday. I'm not going back at all.** I think again of what Aggie would tell me, and I add another **I'm sorry** because you can probably never say it too many times.

Then I get back in my car and drive home.

***

The only light on at the farmhouse is the one over the front door.

I know I could rattle stones at Aggie and Brody's window. I could even tiptoe up the stairs and wake her up.

Despite our differences, I know Aggie wants me to find Gus tonight — to make things right with him.

But I also know she doesn't get enough sleep, and she has things to deal with in her own family. Part of me also knows, as much as I'd definitely rush straight out to Gus's house, even though it's no longer "today" but is now the early hours of "tomorrow," that's possibly not the best decision.

Presumably Gus left because he needs distance. We could both use perspective. Everybody needs to sleep.

With those wise words in my head, I don't sleep.

I walk to the barn which would probably have soothed me if it was full of horses, but with the stalls empty and the aisle swept clean it doesn't help. Whoever first built this barn over a hundred years ago situated it to catch the best of any breeze on offer, and I remember many summer days standing in the doorway feeling five degrees cooler than outside as the air currents swirled around me.

Tonight, even though a welcome wind's come up after the day's stillness, it's fussy and changeable.

The barn is stuffy. I look for the horses, but don't even get the reward of catching a glimpse of dark grazing outlines.

Halfway back to the trailer the coyote yips start. They share the characteristic with tonight's breeze of sounding like they're coming from everywhere. The woodlot behind the farmhouse. The scrub land beyond the trailer. The horses' pasture behind me.

I'm not worried about the horses — one swift kick is enough to take care of any coyote who ventures too close — but when the pack joins together and lifts their voices in a long howl, I decide it's time for me to get inside, even if it is inside the thin metal skin of the trailer.

As I'm stepping through the trailer door there's a rumble from … somewhere. The air all around me fills with thunder and my ears pop.

Inside, I stand with the lights out and, after a few seconds, a flash of lightning outside illuminates the trailer.

Right, so I'm probably not going to be able to sleep with that going on. I need to do something mindless — sleep-inducing — but the festival books are as up-to-date as they'll ever be. My inbox, however, has the most unread messages in it I've ever seen.

I sigh. It's been a shitty night already, so why not?

At least I can delete all the emails from Devon. We've sorted things out. That feels good.

It still leaves a pretty high number of emails from Tom. With a sense of resignation I begin to read his thoughts since I walked out of his life.

***

I sit in the dark, with the flashes from outside reminding me the night's as unsettled as I am.

As I read Tom's emails, my shoulders hunch. My jaw clenches. More than that, though, an old feeling seeps back in — one I never realized I used to carry around. It's a faint background combination of stress and dread. It's like white noise — I can't put my finger on it, but it's definitely there.

Now I'm wondering if what I was experiencing before — that thing I called nostalgia — was also a desire to escape from this oppressive sensation. As though glimmers of a simpler, happier existence were shining through the tension of my West Coast life, promising if I just left — if I drove halfway across the country, I could have it.

And, interestingly, those waves of whatever-it-was have diminished steadily while I've been here, and I haven't felt one for some time.

It's probably just as well I didn't read Tom's emails as they came in, because I would have had to sit with each one as they arrived, and the first ones are pretty angry.

Or, at first I think they're angry. After I read a few, a pattern emerges. **How can you just walk away from me?** leads to, **What am I supposed to say to my boss — he scheduled after-work drinks to celebrate our engagement**, then, **My Aunt Vanessa and Uncle Edward already sent a gift — it's humiliating to have to return it.**

Although they're punctuated by words like "selfish" and "heartless" ("bitch" even makes an appearance once) they're much more about Tom than about me. I made *him* look bad. I made *him* feel stupid.

Something changes after the first few days. It's subtle — because the messages are still about Tom — but now they include specific complaints. **I can't believe you took the clothes steamer, I don't know which day is garbage day, The dog is driving me crazy.**

There's quite a bit about the dog. I never liked her, but I didn't dislike her as much as Tom seems to based on the multiple complaints about her picky eating, refusal to poop in one corner of the yard, growling when he tries to move her from his seat on the couch, and lying down (and refusing to get up) when he attempts to walk her.

About a week after I left, he sends a message saying, **I don't know why I'm emailing you — you're not even bothering to answer.**

Neither do I, Tom. Neither do I.

This is when the first message from my mother peppers into my inbox. **Why isn't there a liner for your shower curtain, Hazel? It's most unusual. I'm not even sure if I'm using it properly.**

Improper use of a shower curtain — there's something I've never considered.

I noticed the elastic on one corner of your mattress cover has let go. I'll buy you a new one. Don't worry — you don't have to pay me back.

You don't seem to have dessert plates. There are salad plates and saucers, but no dessert plates.

Honestly, with all the trials and tribulations, I'm surprised she's stayed there. My fingers are itching to send her a message telling her so.

Fortunately for her, there are a few bright spots. **Paisley has been so helpful. You know what a dependable girl I think she is.** I do, indeed. My mother once described Paisley as "not much to look at, but terribly well-mannered." Paisley will never hear about that description from me.

Your downstairs neighbour, Ruth, is a first-rate woman. We've been having coffee together every morning. She says you can sometimes be quite noisy, Hazel.

Yes, and Ruth is sometimes quite bitchy. She's called the superintendent more than once to complain about the noise of me setting my grocery bags on the floor when I come in from the store.

My ears popping again force me to take a break from my reading. A burst of wind rattles the window screen and skitters something against the trailer siding — dust, leaves? There's another flash of lightning and another roll of thunder. I wish whatever's brewing would just open up.

I shake my head and focus back on the next email. It's from Tom again, and this time something's clearly changed. The self-pity's gone, and the complaining has ended. Tom is now a man with a plan. Hazel, since it's clear we're not getting married, you definitely owe me the engagement ring back — it was a gift conditional on the marriage contract which will not be fulfilled. I've managed to talk the venue into releasing our date without holding back a deposit, so I got you off the hook there. In return, I believe you should take the dog. I can't keep her here — she's a burden and she's unhappy. If you're going to cut me free, that includes looking after the dog. As you should remember, I'm going to my sister's wedding in Toronto. I'll detour to your farm to drop her off and get the ring.

Whoa.

For a second I think Tom must have made the trek down to the family law department in his firm. The whole "conditional gift" assertion tracks with that. Having said that, the second part of his argument definitely strays from logic and reason. There's a whiff of entitlement about it. It reminds me of ...

Of course.

The next message is from my mother. Tom came by the apartment ...

I should have known.

He's a lovely person.

Of course she thinks he is.

You've been quite unreasonable.

It's definitely normal for a mother to take her daughter's ex-fiancé's side.

I've given him the address of the farm so he can return the dog.

The dog. *Return* the dog. How did something that was never my responsibility in the first place, become something to be returned to me?

The final email from my mother reads, When are you coming back, Hazel? Only, Ruth has asked me to attend a

Masterworks concert at the Symphony Orchestra and I feel rude for leaving her hanging.

A yawn hits me as I'm filled with the same-old-same-old weariness of realizing that my mother will always care more for the opinion of somebody she's met a week ago, than she will for the actual predicaments in her children's lives.

In the morning I need to intercept Tom before he gets any ideas about bringing the dog to Ontario. At some point I need to talk to my mother about how long her stay in my condo will last.

Then three things happen in quick succession. A brilliant, flickering jolt of white light. An immense crack of thunder I can feel in my chest. A sound like sheets of water being dropped on the trailer all at once.

I instantly feel the lick of cold air pushing through the open windows and I run to close them against the teeming rain.

It might seem strange to believe I can finally get some sleep right in the middle of a raging storm, but for me it's better than the tension I've been living with all night.

At least something's happening.

I check my phone one last time for a reply from Gus and, finding none, shut it off and tumble into bed where, sure enough, the thrumming of the rain, punctuated by the intervals of lightning-and-thunder noise and light, lull me to sleep in no time.

Seventeen

A LONG, RINGING WHINNY wakes me up. It seems like a good omen.

The trailer's full of pre-sunrise half-light and while it's easy to believe no humans are up yet, the bird, and frog, and insect songs tell me the animal world is fully awake.

Fifteen minutes later I'm in the sand ring with Banks. No phone, no stirrups, and no worries. All my concentration is on extension and collection. Lateral moves. General obedience. I have an idea, but he needs to pass this test before I can move forward with it.

He's good. He's better than I thought or expected. Of course, it's easy to say that in the beautiful still of the morning — no people or activities to distract him. Then again, when Cressy lifts her head and gives a repeat of the whinny that woke me up, he doesn't react. It's something, anyway.

When I'm done riding him, I find some thinning shears hanging on a hook in the tack room and tidy up his mane.

Once he's turned out I return to the tack room and take stock of everything in there. The state of the equipment. What needs laundering. I give Banks' saddle a good clean, removing the stirrups and scrubbing the treads.

I'm procrastinating. All that nervous energy that sent me belting around the County, taking photos in the dark, has turned to just-plain nerves. As much as I wanted to find Gus last night, now I'm afraid to see him, in case he doesn't want to see me.

I know it's wrong. I know it's dumb. I know I have to face it eventually.

I'm dumping out the dirty stirrup-scrubbing water when footsteps slapping on the path snap me to attention.

"Violet?"

She's running. Face flushed. When she reaches me, she bends over double and I can see her ribs heaving under her thin t-shirt. "What is it?" Fear stabs me. Patrick cut himself again. Brody's had an accident in the fields.

"Mom sent me," my niece pants. "Gus is here. She said you should know right away."

"I ..." Excitement does battle with reluctance. I gesture back to the tack room which I was just beginning to put back to rights after pulling out equipment and rooting through trunks.

"I'll do it," Violet says. "You go!"

I bite my lip.

"What are you waiting for?" she stamps her foot. "I didn't run all the way here for you to just stand around. And anyway, you love Gus."

"That's a bold statement."

She shrugs. "You said it."

"I never ..."

"On the way to Toronto, right after I first saw the CN Tower, you said, 'Violet, I love him.'"

I vaguely remember now. Although, of course, she's conveniently left out the middle part of the statement — "Violet, if he makes you happy, I love him" — still, does it really matter? I think I probably do love him.

I wrinkle my nose. "I messed up with that phone call last night."

She shakes her head. "*I* did. I shouldn't have said the whole message out loud in front of Gus. It was my fault he got mad and left."

Aah. So he did get mad and leave. I mean, I knew it, but a tiny part of me still held out hope that he ran off to deal with some emergency that had nothing at all to do with me.

"Actually, not mad," Violet corrects. "Sad. He looked *sad*. He wants you to stay, Auntie Hazel. We all do."

I look down at my shirt, which is the one I slept in. I run my hand through my hair. I think that *no phone* and *no stirrups* extends to *no shower* and *no hairbrush*. "I'm not looking my best self, Vi."

She snorts. "Gus doesn't care about stuff like that — he teaches Seb Granger, who always has snot running out of his nose, and he still likes him."

It's not exactly the reassurance I was looking for, but it'll have to do. I give my nose a quick swipe to make sure at least there's no snot there, hand the bucket to Violet, and go.

***

I trip on the path. Then trip again. I'm clumsy with nerves. Gawkish with excitement. Unable to hold on to grace, or poise, or restraint at the prospect of seeing Gus.

When I round the final bend I can see to the parking area where, sure enough, a big grey pickup sits. This time it just *has* to be his.

The house comes into view and he's standing there, holding a steaming mug, talking to Aggie, and I open my mouth to yell, when a yapping bark grabs my attention, followed by a furry body running a corkscrew pattern around my feet.

My heart freezes. *Oh. My. God.* It's Muffkins.

I look up and, sure enough, standing at the back of Gus's truck, watching the dog assail me, is Tom.

Shoot. Sugar. Shinsplints. Shipwreck.

If the suggestion that I hadn't quite quit my job was enough to send Gus off last night, what will the appearance of my fiancé do? Not to mention the dog, who's whining, and wagging her tail, and pawing at me like I'm her long-lost favourite-person-on-earth.

Living alone with Tom must have been really crappy for her to be this happy to see me.

Here's the problem with the ongoing yipping, and squealing, and whining — Aggie and Gus are both staring at me as I try to walk forward without tripping over the dog's long, low, wriggling body.

Gus has turned to face me, and even from here I can see his knitted brows. Behind him Aggie's gesticulating and mouthing *What the ...?*

I lift my hand. "Hey! Just give me a minute — I'll be right there!" I manage to take one big step over the dog's body and nearly sprint to Tom.

"What are you doing here!" I hiss.

"You'd know if you answered your messages."

"Oh for flip's sake! You can't be here. I can't deal with this."

Tom lifts both hands and doesn't bother to state the obvious. He is here. I do have to deal with it.

The dog has caught up and is licking manure off my paddock boots.

Think, I order myself. *Contain this. Spin it. You're supposed to be good at this.*

I lock my eyes onto Tom's. "I was wrong. I treated you badly. I shouldn't have just left like that. You didn't deserve it." His eyes widen, then narrow as I talk. A thin smile begins to creep across his face. "Now, please, please, please just go away quietly."

The smile straightens. He crosses his arms. "Why would I do that?"

"I'll keep the dog." I look down at my shiny wet paddock boot and wonder how much horse poop she's ingested. *Charming.* "You won't be stuck with her — you can just walk away and forget about her."

He taps his foot. "Well, considering all the countryside around here, I'm not sure there's any need for me to be stuck with her if you don't take her. You never told me your childhood home was quite so rural."

Wow. I was going to marry a guy who would abandon a defenceless city dog on a remote rural road. *Nice.*

I suddenly remember the email thread. "I'll give you the ring."

"This is starting to sound interesting."

"Also the earrings you gave me for my birthday."

He holds his hand out flat toward me.

"They're in my bedroom." I don't trust him enough to let him know that's in the trailer — I can see him deciding to just help himself.

"Go get them."

"Get in your car, pull up to that trailer. Keep the engine running, roll down your window and I'll hand them to you, then you just keep going."

He purses his lips. "I'm not sure."

"Fine." I pick the dog up around her very long midsection. "Here. Take her. Just make sure nobody sees you abandoning her because most people around here carry guns in their trucks —" that's a total lie, but he doesn't need to know that "— and they don't take kindly to animal cruelty. And, as to the ring, considering it was custom-designed for me, I think it was an absolute gift — not a conditional one — so we can discuss that in court if you like."

"You're such a bitch," Tom says.

"Around here, we prefer the term 'witch'."

"What?"

"Just follow me and don't talk to anyone, and you'll be out of here in less than five minutes with no dog and some jewelry."

***

I'm in the trailer for less than thirty seconds, but when I come out chaos has descended.

The dog's on the steps, scratching at the door. Tom's idling just a few feet away, with his hand poised over the horn. A quick glance tells me Gus and Aggie are walking toward the trailer — Aggie hanging back, Gus striding forward — and on top of it all, Ali suddenly appears, squealing, "Dog!"

She drops to the ground and the dog decides the nine-year-old in the swirly skirt is a better bet than me. While they're both distracted, and Aggie and Gus are still about fifty metres away, I drop the ring and earrings into Tom's hand. "There. You can go now."

He hesitates and I know him well enough to see he's conflicted at getting what he wants, while not being able to gloat about it.

It would be just like Tom to stick around for a while longer just for the satisfaction of stirring some shit.

Reminding him of our deal won't help. Instead, I need to play dirty.

I lean into the window. "See that guy walking up behind us? That was his truck you parked beside. He loves his truck and he's not afraid to fight. If you don't put this car in drive right now, I'm going to yell that you hit his truck when you parked."

"But, I didn't!"

"He won't check before he hits you." I tap the roof of Tom's car as I straighten.

"I'm so much better off without you." Tom says, then accelerates away as quickly as a rental Hyundai can.

I watch him go, and remember why I left Vancouver in the first place.

"What's going on?" Gus asks.

"Where did this dog come from?" Ali asks. "Can I keep her?"

Then Patrick joins the fray. "Was that the man you were going to marry, Auntie Hazel?"

Ali snorts. "Don't be stupid. She's going to marry Gus. Right?" Her eyes dart from me to Gus and back again.

I lock eyes with Gus and I see confusion, and frustration, and uncertainty. "Well, honey, I was thinking Gus and I might skip straight to having a honeymoon if that's OK with him."

He blinks. He looks away from me. He shakes his head. When he looks back, there's a twinkle in his eye.

You, he mouths.

You and me, I mouth back.

"Oh, yeah!" Ali yells. "I think Auntie Hazel and Gus are going to have a honeymoon! That's OK, Patrick and I will look after the dog!"

The two kids run off with the dog scampering between them, which leaves Gus and me staring at each other and Aggie standing watching.

"Um, yes. OK. Right. I'll be off."

"Thanks Aggie," I say without looking at her.

"I'll keep the kids away."

"That's great, Ags. Much appreciated." I take one step up toward the trailer door and Gus presses in close against me.

"And, um, if the trailer's rocking, I won't come a ..."

"Aggie!" I give her a quick nod. "I've really come to love you this last little while, and now I need you to go away."

She giggles, and wiggles her fingers, and says, "Bye!" and finally, finally, it's just Gus and me and the trailer.

Eighteen

"I'M SORRY ABOUT THE PHONE CALL," I mumble it into his neck.

"*Just* the phone call?" His voice rumbles through his chest so I feel, more than hear his words.

"I'm sorry about everything." I've found the hem of his shirt and am yanking it up. "Honestly, I'll be sorry about anything you want me to be if you'll just help me get this shirt off you."

With his shirt tossed on the bed I pause for a minute to admire the way the morning sun filters across his much-more-like-a-carpenter-than-a-teacher-abs. They *are* quite nice.

"I'm sorry, too." he says.

I tear my eyes up to his. "Excuse me?"

"You heard me."

"Hmm ... the thing is when you said it the first time, I had this urge to take my shirt off."

"Aah, in that case, *I'm sorry*." Now he reaches for my hem. "Really sorry. Incredibly sorry."

I push my bare chest to his. I never thought I'd be able to bear being hot again, but the warmth of his skin against mine is thrilling. "For what?"

"For leaving before we had a chance to do this last night."

I unbutton his jeans, wiggle my hand down the front of them. "When you say, 'this' ...?"

He shimmies his hands under the stretch of my yoga pants, scoops one of my butt cheeks into each of his hands, "I mean *this*," he says.

I stagger back, let the mattress buckle my knees, fall onto the bed and pull him with me. "This is good."

We don't say much else. The kissing takes care of that.

For what feels like a long time, that's all we do. His cheeks are scratchy, his lips are soft. His rhythm switches between slow and lingering and quick and urgent.

It's heavenly. If all couples could always kiss like this nobody would ever fall out of love.

Soon, though, I want more. I want everything — all of him. I wrap both legs around one of his thighs and squeeze.

"Is there something I can help you with?" he mumbles between kisses.

Rubbing against the lean muscles of his leg feels good ... but not good enough. "Yes, you see, I have this itch."

"What kind of itch?"

"An itch only you can scratch."

He holds up his hand. "With this?"

"That'll do for a start."

Honestly, it's nearly the end of me. His mouth on mine, his long body pressed to me, his fingers inside me, and the added bonus of the relief of being here, with him. Of having a chance to build — whatever this might grow into — with a truly nice, smart, fun person.

It's a lot. It's nearly too much. "Aah ..." I arch my back. "I think we'd better move on or I might not be able to."

He laughs. "Wait, I thought it was only guys who needed a break. I thought you women could just keep going, and going, and going ... or should I say, coming, and ..."

"Not this time. This time I'm going to be a quivering wreck afterwards. Unable to function for quite some time. So, your choice."

He grins and bends to kiss me. He takes his hands away from me and I hear the tear of a wrapper. I'm about to complain about the lost contact when one hand slides up my side and, more importantly, he slides himself inside me. "This is my choice."

"Good one," I say. It's been a long time, and he's possibly very aroused, or possibly just quite well-endowed, but either way the pressure is amazing. "Good one," I repeat. Then, as I move my hips with him, and he gives one particularly, long, slow, deep thrust, "Good one!" after which I fling my arms out and give in to being a quivering wreck.

***

Everyone's excited.

We wake up to the kids' voices. "Get up! Get up! Get up! It's festival day! It's time to go! It's time to get up!"

They overlap — Violet's sweet-but-with the tiniest teenage twang creeping in. Patrick's and Ali's still childish, almost indistinguishable unless you happen to be familiar with the faint growl in Ali's voice that makes me love listening to her.

There's a poke in my side and I roll over to face Gus. "That had better be your finger."

"Oh yeah, not up to another go-round this morning?"

"Don't underestimate me," I say. "It's just that if you start we won't be getting to the festival on time."

He leans forward, kisses my cheek, and breathes in my ear. "I like your attitude."

"I like you." It might not seem like much, but to me it feels like a big admission. It's the most simple and straightforward thing it's possible to say. It doesn't hold anything back. It's not clever, or sassy. It's just out there, with nothing to hide behind.

"I like *you*." I like the way Gus says it. Not an automatic, snap-back, I-like-you-too, but with an emphasis on the "you." Or was it the "like?" Either way, it sends a warm feeling through my core that isn't lust.

Or, at least, isn't only lust.

"Here's the thing, though," I say. "I'm not sure Aggie would appreciate it if we let the kids know just exactly how much we like each other."

"Ah," he says. "So you're suggesting I shouldn't go to the trailer door in my boxers and wish them good morning?"

I try not to be distracted by the fact that he's actually not wearing boxers. "Preferably not."

"Fair enough. I have teacher cred to uphold, anyway."

"What's teacher cred?"

"I shouldn't really have a life outside the classroom."

"They know you have a life outside the classroom, since you live a lot of it here."

He taps the side of his nose. "But they think that's all because I like hanging out with them."

"Right. OK. Not sure I entirely follow your logic but if it keeps you from flashing my nieces and nephew, then all good."

"I was never going to flash them ..."

"Yoo-hoo! Auntie Ha-zel! Are you ever getting up?"

The little voices are really quite close now. Pretty much right under the open window from what I can tell.

"Um, yes!" I call. "I'm just going to have a shower, then make my bed and I'll meet you in the house for breakfast."

"It would be quicker if Gus made the bed while you were in the shower!" I'm pretty sure the voice is Ali's, but it doesn't matter because she's quickly backed up by the other two, adding, "Yes, Gus should make the bed," "Gus, you make the bed."

I open my eyes wide, then blink frantically at Gus before calling through the window. "I know you saw Gus walk me to the trailer last night after dinner, but ..."

"Auntie Hazel?" This time the voice is Violet's.

"Yes?"

"Gus's truck is here."

"Gus's truck ..." my voice comes out weak, partly because I'm marveling at my own stupidity, partly because Gus's eyes are on mine, and he's grinning, then laughing, and I can feel the giggles rising in me.

"A-plus for observation, Violet," Gus calls out the window.

"Thanks!" she calls back. "I learned it in your science class. I also learned how to tell time, and I'm telling both of you to get your butts in gear!"

"Violet! What would your mother say if she knew you were talking about my butt?" I ask.

The only reply is a chorus of giggles, followed by shouts of "Hurry!" "We're going to eat all the Lucky Charms!" "See you in the house!" which I can't answer because Gus is cupping my butt and murmuring, "You heard them. Come on — get this in gear."

Nineteen

IF THIS DAY WAS A GLASS OF WINE, this would be its tasting note:

Bright skies, sun, and moods lead to crowds along the parade route, line-ups for the vendors, and the overall impression that there's never been another festival day quite like this — at least not since last year. Toddler temper tantrums and over-excited dogs are easily dismissed as part of the experience. Tomorrow there will be sunburns to soothe, garbage to pick up, and more than one local-winery-induced hangover to nurse, but everybody will agree days like this are few and far between and it was definitely worth it.

It *is* worth it. I'm sure of that. I do the scan that's become automatic over the last half-hour. I was never a lifeguard, but this must be what it would be like to be one.

Patrick. *Check.* Carried proudly and safely by Milford, with each hoof placed carefully. And those hooves ... spotless and oiled. The arch in the pony's neck emphasized by a neat row of tiny, even plaits. His coat gleaming in the late-August sun which picks out the perfectly executed shark's teeth quarter marks on his fiery chestnut rump.

I apologized to Marta. I also paid her to spend several hours in the barn yesterday and to come back this morning after Gus left.

That's why not only does Milford look great, but our whole crew is immaculately turned out, with coats, hooves, and tack shining, leather and horse hair laying flat, and the final perfect touches of matching quarter marks and matching quarter-zip shirts reading **Edwards Farm** courtesy of Trent's one-day t-shirt printer.

The marks don't show up as well on Cressy's grey backside, but that doesn't really matter since the bloom of her dapples is dazzling enough. As is Ali's tie-dyed skirt draped over her saddle.

The deep bay of Quin's coat, and the inky intensity of Banks's, make the art on their hindquarters pop, and every now and then I catch Violet twisting around in her saddle to admire Quin's.

That's fine with my reliable mature boy. He doesn't mind when people clap, and whoop, and take pictures. He isn't bothered by the runners, darting back and forth through the parade participants handing candies out to spectators on both sides of the road. And, every time the high school marching band strikes up a new song, he just flicks his ears back, then forward again, and keeps walking calmly behind the big trailer, loaded with bus shelters, towed behind my brother's tractor.

Funnily enough, through all the festival planning, I haven't really taken time to study the shelters themselves. The ones on the trailer in front of us are captivating, though. They follow an official "Celebrate the County" theme. One, of course, is in the shape of a bottle of wine – Pinot Noir to be exact – one of the most recognized County varieties and, as a complement, the hut beside it looks like a bottle of cider, made from the County's famous apple orchards. There's a beach-themed hut in honour of the long, sweeping crescent of fine white sand that drew visitors here long before there were wineries. Another hut is decorated to look like the tall, brick, heritage building which is the tallest structure in the County. Once my parade duties are over, I'm looking forward to checking out more of the bus huts at the County commons.

For now, though, I'm still responsible for our little equine foursome. I'm lucky that Milford, Cressy, and Quin are so sweet, and clever, and good-natured, that my nieces and nephew can soak up the attention of the crowd – holding their reins with one hand, waving, giving their mother plenty of opportunities to take great pictures as she scampers along the road, getting ahead of us to establish a good vantage point and snap away.

Banks is doing just fine as well. The more I get to know him, the more I think all he needs is to have his brain occupied. He gives the most trouble when he's bored. Here, today, with the music, and people, and dogs, and strollers, and tractors, and … everything, there's never a dull moment and Banks is taking it all in.

Sure, every now and then – when the parade gets backed up and we have to stand and wait for a bit – he gives a head toss or a sideways dance, but that makes the ride fun for me, and elicits pointing fingers and comments of "Look at the pretty horse!" from the parade watchers, so it's all good.

As we ride under the big banner that signifies the end of the parade route, I catch sight of Trent, standing next to a videographer. He shoots me a big thumbs up, lifts his hands to the brilliant, clear sky, then swoops his arms wide to the throngs of happy people. *Golden*, he mouths to me.

We ride toward Aggie waiting in the staging area. The kids are hepped up, partly because of their fifteen minutes of fame, mostly because the top of the ferris wheel is visible in the distance and the air smells of cotton candy and caramel popcorn. Both Ali and Patrick are on the ground almost before their ponies come to a full halt. They turn toward the commons with shining eyes.

"Hey, you two!" Violet's voice is sharp. "You can't just leave your ponies."

"*Oh* ..." Patrick starts. Ali jabs him in the side and hisses something in his ear, then walks back to Cressy's side. Her eyes follow all the other parade participants migrating in the direction of the festival activities, but she rolls her shoulders back as she gathers Cressy's reins. "Where's the trailer?"

Aggie steps forward with hands out. "Here. Patrick and Ali, give me your reins."

"What?" Ali asks. "Why?" Patrick says. "What about me?" Violet asks.

"Violet, you give yours to Auntie Hazel." Aggie holds an envelope out to her oldest daughter. "There's twenty dollars for each of you in there. Off you go to the common. Your dad and I will meet you at the judging booth in two hours."

"Really?" The chorus comes from all of them at once.

"Yes, but you all stick together and call if you need anything."

They hug their ponies, then hug their mother, and turn toward the common.

"Hey," she says. "Aren't you forgetting something? Who got you into the parade in the first place?"

Violet's the first one to my side, giving me a quick, but fierce hug. "Thanks Auntie Hazel." I get two more hugs, and two more "Thanks," and Aggie yells, "Don't spend all your money in the first fifteen minutes!" then the two of us are alone with four horses in the rapidly emptying staging ground.

"Alright," I say. "Let's us get these beasts back home."

Aggie shakes her head. "Not 'us.'"

Not "us." I mean, I suppose it only takes one person to unload the horses straight off the trailer and out to the paddock. They're still so clean from Marta's incomparable grooming skills that it's not like they need to be brushed. But still ... I didn't think I'd have to do it alone. I wanted to check out the huts before the judging. I wanted to get a hand-squeezed lemonade. If it wasn't for my hard work, this might be the last festival, and I at least wanted to enjoy it.

I battle the-immature, less-magnanimous, last-word-loving version of myself. *Don't say anything. It's not worth it.* Which is true. There's no need for two people to miss out on part of the festival.

Still. It's hard to stay quiet.

"... no need for both of us to miss out." Well, now, that stings a bit – to have Aggie turn my own argument against me. I open my mouth to ask where I was when the take-the-horses-back-to-the-farm-alone coin toss happened, when I'm stopped by a voice calling, "Yoo-hoo! Sorry I'm late. I was stuck in the line-up for lemonade. So delicious!"

It's Marta, sipping a tall cup of lemonade that looks amazing with the sun's rays slanting through it.

"... ready to go ..." she's saying.

"Great!" Aggie claps her hands. "Hazel, could you maybe just load Banks and Quin while Marta puts her lemonade in the truck? That way she and I can get going and I can be back in lots of time to meet the kids."

Hot shame washes me. "You don't have to. I'll go."

"Of course not. If it wasn't for your hard work this might have been the last festival. You should enjoy it."

I bite my lip. Shake my head.

"What is it?" She's peering at me. "Are you feeling OK? Your cheeks are flushed."

I beckon her closer with my finger and when she leans in, I whisper. "I definitely am not a nice person."

Her brow furrows. "Why?"

"I didn't want to take the horses back to the farm. I thought you were going to send me on my own. I was getting pretty inwardly pissy about it."

She snorts. "Of course you didn't want to go. You have a very hot guy out there somewhere looking for you. I, on the other hand, have the entire farm to myself for a blissful half-hour or so once I've unloaded these horses and sent Marta home." She takes a step closer and, to my shock, kisses me on the cheek. "Listen, Hazel. Neither one of us is perfect. I'm hoping from here on in, we can give each other the benefit of the doubt and have each other's backs."

I nod. "Yeah. I can try that."

"Good. Because ..."

"Because what?"

"Because your mom called this morning and she was talking about Bruce, and I was terrified she was going to tell me she was coming back to see him ..."

I nod. "That is a scary prospect."

"So I said you'd be happy for her to invite Bruce out for a visit, and you don't need your condo anytime soon, and she doesn't have to pay rent ... and I'm sorry, Hazel – I know it's not my condo, and we can use some of the film shoot money to pay your mortgage if you need us to, but I just couldn't ..."

"... face having her back here right now?"

Aggie shakes her head. "Exactly. It's been so nice."

"Ags?"

"Yeah?"

"I agree. It's been great, in fact. And we can't avoid her forever, but I think we deserve a little breathing room."

"So you don't mind?"

I pull her in tight for a hug, and whisper in her ear. "I would have killed you if you'd told me she was coming back."

***

The village common is transformed. Normally a big green space lightly used by dog walkers and kids taking a shortcut from the school to the village candy store, today it's a buzz of activity, a riot of colour, and full of the sounds and smells of the festival.

There are bus shelters everywhere. One looks like the CN Tower. One is a lighthouse. There's one shaped like the sentry huts dotted at sights around downtown Ottawa.

I stop for a moment at one that looks just like the Peace Tower on Parliament Hill. It's really good. Each festival visitor gets a vote for best shelter, and this one might get mine.

There's a little boy peeking out of it. His freckled face and gap-toothed grin look familiar. Then a little girl's face appears beside his. She has the same freckles and bright blue eyes.

Those two kids together ... *no way*. I clue into Kumar, standing off to the side, next to a couple who look both very ordinary – just like any proud mom and dad, smiling as they watch their children – but who are possibly the most famous couple in the country.

I hear the man say to Kumar, "The kids enjoyed it so much last time, we just had to come back." Kumar answers. "We're very glad you did. We hope to see you next year."

Next year. I'm so glad there will be a next year. That reminds me of Trent's company's sponsorship.

I look around for the film crew. I can't decide if I wish they were here to capture the Prime Minister's attendance, or if I'm glad they aren't, to preserve his family's privacy.

The little girl dashes out of the shelter. "Can we go get cotton candy?"

"Of course!" The family walks off and two large men follow them at a discreet distance.

I look at my phone, hovering my finger over Trent's contact info. Text him, or leave it be?

I glance up and all thoughts of Trent, or texting him, leave my mind. I can't even think about the Prime Minister any more.

Because standing in front of me is Gus. And, while it's true my knees go weak and my insides tighten with a twist of lust, my lungs also lose most of their capacity, and my heart beats double-time. I might not have a lot of experience with these things, but I'm almost positive what I'm feeling is lust and love.

God, how do people in love actually function in this world?

"What are you staring at?" he asks.

"All of it," I say. "You've outdone yourself." He's wearing a navy polo shirt and tan chinos. Around his neck is a lanyard, and even though the card on it says **Gimme Shelter Volunteer** I can easily picture one with the logo of the County school board. "There's only one thing, though ..."

"What?"

"No way did that haircut cost you sixteen dollars."

He laughs, and smooths the hair away from each side of its neat part. "Busted. Twenty-one dollars by the time I paid taxes and tip."

I step forward and press myself against him. Run my hands up his back. Whisper in his ear. "The extra five bucks were so worth it."

He places his hands on my shoulders. "Miss Edwards, I'm afraid you're destroying my teacher cred. No life outside the classroom – remember?"

"Right," I say. "That's unfortunate, considering all I want to do is pick up where we left off this morning."

"Well, if you'll just follow me." He takes my hand and begins to walk.

"Where?"

"You'll see."

He leads me past the lemonade stand with its long, long line-up. Past the cotton candy kiosk where the PM's adorable kids are being handed fluffy sugar clouds.

We go by Brenda, clasping a clipboard. Flora talking into a walkie-talkie, and in the distance I see Peace leading a small crowd of visitors through a maze of shelters.

There are many, many signs for toilets, written in childish printing, and I begin to worry that's where Gus is taking me.

We round a towering evergreen, and tucked behind its wide-sweeping branches is a neat little school bus shelter, only this one has a door.

"What ...?" I ask.

Gus doesn't say anything – just taps the sign over the door. I look up and read **The Love Shack.**

The giggles bubble up in me and I'm still laughing when he pulls me in, shuts the door behind us, and puts his mouth on mine.

As I kiss him back, and untuck his polo shirt from his chinos, I'm thinking The Peace Tower has lost my vote.

It's The Love Shack for me.

PLEASE LEAVE A REVIEW!

REVIEWS help me sell books. More sales let me write more books. A simple star rating and a few quick words are all that's needed to help other readers decide if they want to read my books.

To review, please follow this link – https://tinyurl.com/reviewNsB – and select your preferred retailer. Or, use this QR code:

If you liked this book …

… you might enjoy Tudor's other books. Read the beginning of *Before & After*, to find out.

Before & After

Before

The two pictures say it all. Before and after.

Before there are eleven of us. Not a crease or a grass stain in sight. Every hair in place on every head. The flower girl and ring bearer smiling angelic smiles. Slightly blurry in the background and off to the side two of my aunt's near-black Canadians hitched to the wagon that brought the bride to the wedding.

Charlie and Bree are in the centre, of course. Stars of the show. Shining with anticipation … and a few nerves.

On Bree's side Cleo and I smile, wide and genuine. Behind Cleo are Bree's parents – Cleo's grandparents –

looking very similar to Charlie's parents on the other side; as though they're wearing waistbands that cinch and shoes that pinch. Standing unnaturally straight. If you look closely enough you can see the tan line Charlie's dad's baseball cap has left across his forehead.

On Charlie's side is his brother Sam who, truly, is always delighted with life, but looks even more so in the picture, and next to Sam is Dob.

Dob, who stole my heart in grade seven, then broke it at the end of grade eight when he told the rest of us he was going to the technical high school instead of the academic one Charlie and Bree and I went to. It was a pattern the two of us would stick to all through high school and after. Love, then hate. Happy, then sad. Together, then apart. But when that photo was taken, we'd been steadily together for a long time. We shared a too-hot-in-the-summer and too-cold-in-the-winter third-floor apartment. We had jobs and paid our rent. Charlie and Bree had asked us to be their best man and maid-of-honour.

When the wedding photographer jostled us into position for the Before picture I was positive I'd have a ring on my finger by the time she lined us up for the After.

In the After photo there are ten of us.

There are grass stains across the bottom of Bree's dress, and everybody looks a little rumpled. Cleo's updo is down. Both dads' suit jackets are unbuttoned. The flower girl and ring bearer have chocolate rings around their mouths and he's leaning on her, with her scowling at him. Charlie and Bree are beaming with relaxed happiness. Cleo and Sam have the look of people who've done their job well. My smile is tight, and my eyes are focused, not on the bride and groom, but on the space next to Sam where Dob should be.

But isn't.

Oh, and my ring finger is still bare.

Then, and now.

No ring, and no Dob since that day.

If you liked the first part of Before & After, why not read the rest of the book? You can find it using this QR code.

ABOUT THE AUTHOR

TUDOR ROBINS is the author of books that move your heart, mind, and pulse.

A little piece of Tudor's own heart is in many places: the central-Ottawa neighborhood where she lives, the Gatineau hills and Eastern Ontario countryside where she loves to hike, Wolfe Island and the St. Lawrence River where she loves swimming and paddleboarding, and the university towns that are currently home to her children.

When she's not writing, Tudor rides, runs, quilts, and walks with her best friends and her Jack Russell / Potcake mix, Cara.

Please contact Tudor at tudorrobins@gmail.com!